# the greatest stories ever told

# the greatest stories ever told
## volume two

**GREG LAURIE**

# The Greatest Stories Ever Told, *Vol. 2*

Unless otherwise indicated, Scripture quotations are taken from the New King James Version.® Copyright © 1982 by Thomas Nelson, Inc. Used by permission. All rights reserved.

Scripture quotations marked NLT are taken from the Holy Bible, New Living Translation, copyright © 1996, 2004. Used by permission of Tyndale House Publishers, Inc., Carol Stream, Illinois 60188. All rights reserved.

Scripture quotations marked NIV are taken from the Holy Bible, New International Version®. NIV®. Copyright © 1973, 1978, 1984 by International Bible Society. Used by permission of Zondervan. All rights reserved.

Scripture quotations marked "THE MESSAGE" are taken from THE MESSAGE. Copyright © by Eugene H. Peterson 1993, 1994, 1995, 1996, 2000, 2001, 2002. Used by permission of NavPress Publishing Group.

Scripture quotations marked NASB are taken from the NEW AMERICAN STANDARD BIBLE®, Copyright © 1960, 1962, 1963, 1968, 1971, 1972, 1973, 1975, 1977, 1995 by The Lockman Foundation. Used by permission.

Scripture quotations marked (ESV) are from The Holy Bible, English Standard Version, copyright © 2001 by Crossway Bibles, a division of Good News Publishers. Used by permission. All rights reserved.

Scripture quotations marked TLB are taken from The Living Bible copyright © 1971. Used by permission of Tyndale House Publishers, Inc., Carol Stream, Illinois 60188. All rights reserved.

Scripture quotations marked KJV are taken from the Holy Bible, King James Version.

Library of Congress Cataloging-in-Publication Data
1 2 3 4 5 6 7 8 9 10/11 10 09 08 07 06

ISBN: 0–9777103–7–8
Published by: Allen David Publishers—Dana Point, California
Coordination: FM Management, Ltd.
Cover design by Chris Laurie
Designed by Highgate Cross + Cathey
Printed in the United States of America

# contents

## chapter one

# Moses' Story: What God Is Like

"Surely blessing I will bless you, and multiplying
I will multiply you." —Hebrews 6:14

**m**an is incurably religious. Down through the ages, most people have believed in the existence of God or gods. It may be that most human beings have given more attention to this idea of a supreme being or beings than all other concerns—food, clothing, housing, work, pleasure—put together.

The Greeks and Romans had a whole pantheon of gods, with familiar names like Jupiter, Mars, Mercury, and Venus. All of those multiple gods and multiple altars troubled the heart of the apostle Paul on one occasion when he was passing through Athens on his way to Corinth.

With a little time on his hands, the apostle decided to take a walk through town. That's when he saw that the city was filled with images and idols erected to various deities. And it distressed him.

It's easy to understand why. Paul had been a champion of the one true God from childhood. And Athens in that day probably had more temples, shrines, and altars than Los Angeles has McDonalds.

But as common as this belief in some kind of deity or supreme being might be, the nature of who God is and what He is like is a mystery to most people. The first-century Athenians hedged their bets by erecting an altar "to an unknown god." In other words, if there is a god out there that we've missed or overlooked in the religious life of our city, we want to make sure we're covered . . . even though we have no idea of who that particular deity might be.

In Acts 17, Paul seized on that altar to a mystery and set out to declare to them the Good News about this unknown god. With that idea as his on-ramp, he spoke to them about the true and living God who had sent His Son to redeem the world.

# Making God Known

God is still unknown to many people today. They don't know His name, they don't understand His nature, and they can't comprehend His holiness, power, and love.

And that's why God gave us the Bible. From one cover to the other, it was written to tell us what He is like. In fact, that was one of Jesus' principle objectives when He walked on this planet.

John tells us that "No one has ever seen God, but God the One and Only, who is at the Father's side, has made him known." Jesus said, "No one has seen the Father except the one who is from God; only he has seen the Father."[1]

To help people grasp a God they didn't really know or understand, Jesus told stories that illustrated His Father's nature and heart of compassion. In the story of the prodigal son, for example, Jesus tells of a father who longs for fellowship with his ungrateful runaway son, and runs to meet him when the boy comes straggling back home. It's a story that has touched people all over the world for thousands of years.

## "The LORD Bless You . . ."

Some would suggest that the God of the Old Testament is different from the God of the New Testament. Nothing could be further from the truth. From one end of the Bible to the other, we see a God who loves, cares, and remains vitally interested in the course of our lives.

Way back in the book of Numbers, the fourth book of the Bible, we come to a passage that reveals God's heart for His people and gives us yet one more clue of what He is like.

And the LORD spoke to Moses, saying: "Speak to Aaron and his sons, saying, 'This is the way you shall bless the children of Israel. Say to them:

"The LORD bless you and keep you;
The LORD make His face shine upon you,
And be gracious to you;

The LORD lift up His countenance upon you,
And give you peace." '

So they shall put My name on the children of Israel,
and I will bless them." (Numbers 6:22-27)

The book of Numbers is a record of the wanderings of the
Israelites in the wilderness. It tells us of the trials they faced and
the mistakes they made as they traveled to the Promised Land. It
chronicles their rebellion, stubbornness, ingratitude, and complaining—and the ramifications of their disobedience. But it also
shows God's incredible longsuffering and patience with them.

We, too, live in a wilderness. We're travelers passing through
from one place to the next. And we also face our trials and make
our mistakes. In addition to that, we face threats each and every
day. Since 9-11, we all look over our shoulders a bit more. With
the government uncovering more and more terrorism attempts—
and evil plots so hateful and destructive that it boggles the
mind—it can be a bit frightening sometimes.

Then there are all the normal concerns of our lives: our liveli-
hood, health, marriage, children, and future. These concerns only
increase as you get older. The fact is, we are a fallen people living
in a fallen world in need of a little help. Actually, a lot of help.

We need the blessing of our God every bit as much as the ancient Hebrews needed it. That's why God instructed the Israelite
priests to pronounce a special blessing on His people, a people
wandering in the wilderness. He wanted that blessing spoken
again and again. The Lord was saying, "I want this ingrained
in their brains, etched in their hearts. I want them to know this
blessing by memory and be able to recite it at a moment's notice."

Why? Because it reminds us of who God is, what He is like,
and how He sees you and me. There are six truths that shine out
from these verses; six statements that reveal God's heart toward
His own. I am indebted to my friend Damian Kyle for his excellent outline on this text.

# Truth 1: God Loves to Bless You

"The LORD bless you..." (Numbers 6:24)

Christians like to toss around the words "bless" and "blessing." We say it quite a lot, and most of the time we mean it.

We also abuse the term. Sometimes as Christians we use the word to let people know the conversation is over, and that it's time for them to leave. We stand up from our desk, or if we've met someone out in public and we get tired of talking to them, we'll smile and say, "God bless you!" Which, being translated, means: Good-bye. Go away!

Blessing, however, is truly a spiritual term. The world may try to hijack it, but they really have no idea of what it means. In fact, true blessing is something only a child of God can experience.

Jesus both began and concluded His earthly ministry blessing people. After His resurrection, when He met the two downhearted disciples on the road to Emmaus, He blessed them. When children came to Him He took them in His arms and blessed them. Just before He ascended into heaven, Jesus lifted His hands and blessed His followers. Jesus loved to bless people. In a portion of the Sermon on the Mount we call the "Beatitudes," He tied together a whole string of blessings.

> Then He opened His mouth and taught them, saying:
> "Blessed are the poor in spirit,
> For theirs is the kingdom of heaven...."
> (Matthew 5:2-3)

Our word for "blessed" comes from the Greek word *makarios*. In fact, this was the Greek name for the Mediterranean island of Cyprus. Because of its geographical location, balmy climate, and fertile soil, the Greeks believed that anyone who lived on this island had it made in the shade. As far as they were concerned, everything anybody needed for happiness and fulfillment could be found right there, on that sunny island. A self-contained place of happiness. There was no need to import anything, because if you lived in Cyprus, you had it all.

In other words, *makarios* was a metaphor for complete blessedness or happiness. From this, we learn two important things about God and blessings.

First, God wants us to be blessed and happy. He truly does. In the opening chapter of Genesis we read: "So God created Man in His own image; in the image of God . . . He created them." And the very next words are, *"God blessed them."*[2] So just know that the Lord loves to bless us.

Second, blessedness or true happiness is independent from circumstances. The point Jesus is making in Matthew 5 is that blessedness, the happiness that God has for us, is independent of what may be happening in our life at the moment.

So here in Numbers, the Lord tells the priest to do this for His people—to stand before them and say, "the Lord bless you."

Some might feel as though this benediction ought to read, "The Lord curse you . . ." That's because they have lived apart from God's blessings, and feel that they're dealing with His curse on their lives. Is it true that God cursed certain people or places? Yes, it is. But there was always a reason for that. His blessings could not fall on people who rejected His kindness and love. For all practical purposes, they had chosen to be cursed instead.

God cursed Cain because of his disobedience (Genesis 4:11-12). God said there would be a curse on the person who worshipped false gods (Deuteronomy 27:15), and on the person who lived immorally (Deuteronomy 27:20). The list goes on.

But there is one key passage in the book of Deuteronomy that shows us we have a choice between God's blessing or curse.

> I call heaven and earth as witnesses today against you, that
> I have set before you life and death, blessing and cursing;
> therefore choose life, that both you and your descendants
> may live; that you may love the LORD your God, that you
> may obey His voice, and that you may cling to Him,
> for He is your life and the length of your days. . . .
> (Deuteronomy 30:19-20)

For those of us who have chosen life, who have chosen to love Him, cling to Him, and obey His voice, there is blessing. *Blessing in abundance.* Your Father loves to bless you! Jesus said, "Do not fear, little flock; for it is your Father's good pleasure to give you the kingdom."[3]

As a father, it was my joy to bless (some would say spoil) my sons. Looking back, I have to say that it never felt like a "task" or a heavy burden for me to feed or clothe them. You would have never heard me say, "What? More baby food? Do you have any idea how much this is costing?" Or, "Are you kidding? I have to pay for diapers for this kid again?"

It was a privilege and a joy to have my boys in the house, and now I get to experience it all over again as a grandfather (and I don't even have to mess with diapers!).

## Truth 2: God Has Promised to Keep You

"The LORD bless you and keep you . . ." (Numbers 6:24)

God wants us to be constantly reassured that He will keep us and care for us. The Israelites needed to hear that as they moved from place to place in a desolate wilderness. And in the twenty-first century, in such an evil and uncertain world as this, we need this reassurance too.

Sometimes we worry about our safety and security, not only for ourselves but for our families. At other times we worry about our relationship with God, and our personal salvation. Even mature believers experience seasons of doubt. Elijah did. So did Moses, Gideon, Hezekiah, Thomas, and others.

But God promises to *keep* us.

I will lift up my eyes to the hills—
From whence comes my help?
My help comes from the LORD,
Who made heaven and earth.

He will not allow your foot to be moved;
He who keeps you will not slumber.

Behold, He who keeps Israel
Shall neither slumber nor sleep.

The LORD is your keeper;
The LORD is your shade at your right hand.
The sun shall not strike you by day,
Nor the moon by night.

The LORD shall preserve you from all evil;
He shall preserve your soul.
The LORD shall preserve your going out and your coming in
From this time forth, and even forevermore.
(Psalm 121:1-7)

The Hebrew word used for *keep* means "to keep, to watch, to guard, to hedge about."

Remember the story in Job when the angels came to present themselves before the Lord, with Satan among them? God started bragging on His beloved servant, and Satan challenged Him.

Then the LORD said to Satan, "Have you considered My servant Job, that there is none like him on the earth, a blameless and upright man, one who fears God and shuns evil?"

So Satan answered the LORD and said, "Does Job fear God for nothing? *Have You not made a hedge around him, around his household, and around all that he has on every side?* You have blessed the work of his hands, and his possessions have increased in the land." (Job 1:8-10)

Those things are true for you, too. God has put a hedge or wall of protection around your life, one that Satan can neither scale nor penetrate. And if he tries to go in the front door, he has to face the Great Shepherd! Jesus said "I tell you the truth, I am the gate for the sheep. . . . Yes, I am the gate."[4]

Many passages remind us of the keeping power of God.

- 2 Thessalonians 3:3: But the Lord is faithful, who will establish you and guard you from the evil one.

- Jude 1:24: Now to Him who is able to keep you from stumbling, and to present you faultless before the presence of His glory with exceeding joy.

- 1 Peter 1:5: . . . Who are kept by the power of God through faith for salvation ready to be revealed in the last time.

- Jude 1:1: . . . To those who have been called, who are loved by God the Father and kept by Jesus Christ.

When expressing the keeping power of God, the original language uses what Bible scholars call the perfect tense; the nearest equivalent in English is *continually kept.* It is a continuing result of a past action. Because He has decided to keep us, He will carry that commitment forward through all the days and years of our lives.

Whatever your difficulties may be, you need to know that you are preserved in Christ! The apostle John tells us that "Jesus knew that His hour had come that He should depart from this world to the Father, having loved His own who were in the world, He loved them to the end."[5]

You don't lose something that you love. You don't carelessly toss aside your favorite hat or sunglasses or latest cell phone . . . you keep your eye on what you value. You know where it is. You don't go to Disneyland with your kids only to leave them behind and completely forget them. (Although you may be tempted!)

God never forgets what He loves. In the book of Isaiah He says: "Can a mother forget her nursing child? Can she feel no love for the child she has borne? But even if that were possible, I would not forget you! See, I have written your name on the palms of my hands."[6]

He has invested heavily in finding you, saving you, and adopting you into His own family, and He will protect His investment! Were it not for the preserving grace of God, not a single one of us would make it. I don't care how strong you think you are, you would "spiritually vapor-lock" on the spot.

The Bible leaves no doubt: Jesus is always there loving, preserving, and praying for those who belong to Him.

> Therefore he is able to save completely those who come to God through him, because he always lives to intercede for them. (Hebrews 7:25, NIV)

Scripture makes it abundantly clear: You and I are preserved, protected, and continually kept by the power of God.

"So Greg," someone will inevitably ask, "does that mean I can never really fall away from my faith?"

*No.* Actually, you can fall away. In the book of Jude, we are warned and encouraged to "keep yourselves in the love of God."[7] Though God's love is unsought, undeserved, and unconditional, it is possible for you to turn away and fall out of harmony with that love. Here's the way the writer of Hebrews puts it:

> See to it, brothers, that none of you has a sinful, unbelieving heart that turns away from the living God. But encourage one another daily, as long as it is called Today, so that none of you may be hardened by sin's deceitfulness. We have come to share in Christ if we hold firmly till the end the confidence we had at first. (Hebrews 3:12-14, NIV)

So what does Jude mean when he tells us to "keep ourselves in the love of God"? Simply put, it means this: *Keep yourself from all that is unlike Him.* Keep yourself from any influence that violates His love and brings sorrow to His heart. Keep yourself in a place where God can actively demonstrate His love toward you. That means staying away from certain people, places, and activities that make it easier for us to fall into temptation. Now that we've been delivered from the kingdom of Satan, we want to make sure we never place ourselves in his clutches and back under his control.

When we pray (as Jesus taught us), "Lead us not into temptation," we're asking the Father to help us so we won't deliberately place ourselves in volatile situations. Bottom line, if you truly *want* to be kept safe, preserved, and enjoy God's hedge of protection around your life, it's there for you.

Okay, you say, I'm enclosed in the hedge. Does that mean God will keep me from trials, sorrows, and difficulties? No, not at all. If we think the road to heaven is all sunlight and daisies, we'll be thrown for a loop when hardships or tragedies come into our lives. We will incorrectly conclude that God has somehow failed in His promise to keep us. The truth is, God has never promised to keep us from all the bumps, bruises, and heartaches of life in this world. However, even though He may not keep us *from* the hardships, He will keep us *through* the hardships. He will be with us. He will give us His grace. He will see us through.

> When you pass through the waters,
> I will be with you;
> and when you pass through the rivers,
> they will not sweep over you.
> When you walk through the fire,
> you will not be burned;
> the flames will not set you ablaze.
> For I am the LORD, your God,
> the Holy One of Israel, your Savior.
> (Isaiah 43:2-3, NIV)

The Lord didn't say, "*If* you pass through the waters . . . *if* you pass through the rivers . . . *if* you walk through the fire . . ." He said those things will be a part of our lives during our short stay on earth. I'm sure you have already had your personal share of waters, rivers, and fire. And if not, hold on, because you will.

But what a difference to face those things knowing that God is watching over your every step and will keep you in His power and love! He is no less our keeper for allowing difficulty to come our way.

And if we trust Him, He will walk with us and keep us through that difficulty until we reach the other side of it.

When the Israelites came up against the dead end between Pharaoh's army and the Red Sea, they had already been walking in a miracle. With a mighty hand, God had delivered them from centuries of slavery and brought the whole nation out of captivity. When had such a thing ever happened in history?

So the sea stretched out before them, and they could hear the rumble of horses and chariots behind them, as a vengeful Pharaoh and his army were in hot pursuit. Terrified, the Israelites pointed the finger of blame at Moses, crying out, "Why did you bring us out here to die in the wilderness? Weren't there enough graves for us in Egypt? Why did you make us leave? Didn't we tell you to leave us alone while we were still in Egypt? Our Egyptian slavery was far better than dying out here in the wilderness!"

You know the rest of the story. God parted that Red Sea, and the Israelites passed through safely to the other side. Then those same parted waters crashed down on the Egyptian army, drowning them.

Why didn't God just lift up the whole nation and teleport them to the other side? Because then they (and we) wouldn't have learned a priceless lesson: While God may not keep us *from* the trial, He will show His power and love by keeping us *through* the trial.

The same is true with those three courageous Hebrew teens, Shadrach, Meshach, and Abendego. They not only had to face the possibility of execution by fire in the king's blazing furnace, they actually had the experience of being tossed alive into those hungry flames.

I love what happened next. It has to be one of my favorite stories in the Bible:

Then King Nebuchadnezzar was astonished; and he rose in haste and spoke, saying to his counselors, "Did we not cast three men bound into the midst of the fire?"

They answered and said to the king, "True, O king."

"Look!" he answered, "I see four men loose, walking in the midst of the fire; and they are not hurt, and the form of the fourth is like the Son of God." (Daniel 3:24-25)

It wasn't just three individuals walking through the fire that day; there was a fourth, and that fourth was the Son of God. In the same way, He will keep us through our trials, no matter how fiery.

There are so many illustrations of this principle. Right off the top of the head we could name Noah and the flood, Jonah and the great fish, Daniel and the lion's den.

"Yes," you say, "but it isn't always a happy ending. John the Baptizer got beheaded. Herod killed James with a sword. Stephen was stoned to death. Where was the keeping power of God for them? Or what about when a godly man or woman is hurt or killed in a terrible accident, or stricken with a massive heart attack? Has God failed to keep them?

In even asking a question like that, we are assuming it is somehow our right to live long, easy, and relatively tranquil lives and die peacefully in our sleep one day. But that's not what the Bible says. Jesus did not say, "In this world you will only have blue skies and sunshine." Rather He said, "In this world you will have tribulation, but be of good cheer . . ."[8]

Whatever happens in our lives, "our times are in His hands." Our life is a gift to us from God right now, and that breath you just took was a gift as well. Don't take that for granted. Even death doesn't mean God has somehow failed in His promise to keep us. Barring the Rapture, that great event in which Jesus Christ will return for His Church, there will come a time for each one of us to make that journey home to Heaven.

And when that moment comes, *however* it comes, God will be right there, taking us by the hand and guiding us from one life to the next.

So far we've seen that God wants to bless you, and that He will keep you. But there's a third truth to consider here.

## Truth 3: God Smiles on You

"The LORD make His face shine upon you . . ." (Numbers 6:25)

God wants us to be reminded daily that when He looks on us, He smiles! That's what this text means.

That's not the picture many people have of the Lord. They see Him as a frowning, glowering Father in Heaven, looking down on us with arms folded and one foot impatiently tapping, rarely if ever pleased by us. But that is not the picture God gives us of Himself.

God's face shines with pleasure toward us as His people. When He sees you, His face just lights up with joy! He isn't angry with you and He isn't disappointed with you.

> He is merciful and tender toward those who don't deserve it; he is slow to get angry and full of kindness and love. (Psalm 103:8, TLB)

He isn't a God who is by nature grumpy and unhappy with us until we do something nice to change His mood. He loves us, and the very thought of us, the very sight of us, puts a smile on His face.

When you read about the ancient religions, you encounter angry, fickle deities. There was no pleasing them. They always had a chip on their shoulders, and you had to walk on eggshells around them. You never knew on what side of the bed they'd be getting up from morning by morning.

But through this blessing in the book of Numbers, the Lord was basically saying, "I want my people to know on a regular basis that I am not like that!"

Paul writes: "What then shall we say to these things? If God is for us, who can be against us? He who did not spare His own Son, but delivered Him up for us all, how shall He not with Him also freely give us all things?"[9]

Not only does God's smiling, shining face look at you, but He *sings* over you as well! Consider this amazing passage:

> The LORD your God in your midst,
> The Mighty One, will save;
> He will rejoice over you with gladness,
> He will quiet you with His love,
> He will rejoice over you with singing.
> (Zephaniah 3:17)

I wonder what God's voice sounds like. As the prophet Ezekiel was describing a vision of the glory of the Lord, he wrote that "His voice was like the roar of rushing waters."[10]

I've always loved the ocean. The very sound of it calms me. God's voice is like the roar of rushing waters, or maybe the crash of the surf on a moonlit beach.

## Truth 4: God Is Gracious to You

"The LORD make His face shine upon you,
And be gracious to you . . ." (Numbers 6:25)

This is also something He wants us to be reminded of. It's important that we understand what grace is—God's unmerited favor. We might better understand it by contrasting it with two other words: *justice* and *mercy*.

*Justice* is getting what I deserve.

*Mercy* is not getting what I deserve.

*Grace* is getting what I don't deserve.

Let's say I loaned my Harley to a friend one weekend, and he crashed and totaled it. Well, that friend of mine owes me a new bike! That's what justice demands. But let's say I decided to be merciful instead of demanding justice. In that case, I would ask for nothing in return; I would simply pardon him. But if I dealt with him in grace, I would take him out to dinner, then go to the Harley dealer afterwards and *buy him* a brand new Harley of his own.

You say, that sounds a little extravagant. And yet it is *nothing* compared with what the Lord has done for you and me.

We deserve hell, and we get heaven.

We deserve punishment, and we get rewards.

We deserve wrath, and we get love.

We deserve exile, and we get adopted into God's own family.

The Lord is gracious unto you! How we need His grace on a daily, even moment by moment basis. Why? Because we sin each and every day. Sins of omission and commission—things I've done that I shouldn't have done, and things that I should have done but didn't! That is why Jesus taught us to pray in the Lord's Prayer: "Forgive us our sins as we forgive those who sinned against us."

We know that prayer is a daily prayer because it includes, "Give us this day our daily bread." Just as surely as we need God's physical provisions every day, so we also need His forgiveness every day. We are essentially praying, "Lord, extend Your grace to me today."

This is how we are saved in the first place . . . by His grace.

> For by grace you have been saved through faith, and that not of yourselves; it is the gift of God, not of works, lest anyone should boast. (Ephesians 2:8-9)

His grace is also that which surrounds us and preserves us each day. When Paul felt he couldn't go on, praying and pleading for the removal of an agonizing burden in his life, God replied, "My grace is sufficient for you, for My strength is made perfect in weakness."[11]

At the beginning of this chapter, I mentioned the story of the prodigal son. I think it must be one of the most beautiful illustrations of God's graciousness in all of Scripture. If the father in Jesus' parable had been just, he would have had the boy stoned to death. If he was merely merciful, he would have taken him on as a hired hand, as the young man requested. But the father's response went beyond justice and beyond mercy . . . all the way to grace. He ran to meet the dirty, emaciated young man, and walked him back home again with a smile of pure joy on his face.

So God blesses, keep, smiles, and is gracious to us. And if all of those things weren't enough, there's yet another truth here.

## Truth 5: God Is Attentive to You

"The LORD lift up His countenance upon you . . ." (Numbers 6:26)

What does that mean, that He lifts up His countenance? It literally means that He lifts up His face to look at me, to see my situation, to have a keen interest and give full attention to what's going on in my life.

Incredible! God is saying, "I watch out for you each and every day, and you have My full attention."

Have you ever been speaking to someone and pouring out your heart and suddenly you notice that they're looking right past you? Now, that is disheartening. It makes you feel a little bit devalued, doesn't it? Sometimes we may imagine that's how it is with God. He seems to be looking our way, but then we begin to wonder if His eyes are roaming somewhere else in the universe. Maybe there's a huge supernova going on in the Andromeda galaxy, and He wants to check it out. Or maybe something big is coming down in the Middle East, and His attention is diverted. Finally He looks back at us and says, "Now, what were you saying?"

Does He truly pay attention to me? Does He really know what's happening in my life right now—what I'm feeling, what I'm wondering, what I'm worried about?

The Lord doesn't want us to be concerned about such things. God is a Father who "lifts up His countenance" to us. He looks at us face to face, eye to eye. He gives us His full attention.

Isn't that one of the essential messages of Christmas? As Matthew recorded for us: "'Behold, the virgin shall be with child, and bear a Son, and they shall call His name Immanuel,' which is translated, God with us."[12]

He is *your* Immanuel . . . He is the God with *you*.

You may be at a place in your life where you've convinced yourself that no one really cares about what you think or feel or dream. But God does. You have His full attention.

Do you suppose Joseph felt God was attentive to him as he sat for two years in that Egyptian dungeon, falsely accused of rape? As the days ran on and on, it must have seemed at times that God didn't care at all. But the fact is, God was watching and attentive every moment. The Lord had incredible plans for this young man's life. Although Joseph couldn't have known it at the time, the Lord was about to make him the second most powerful man on Earth.

In order to prepare Joseph for this crucial role on the world stage, God allowed some time, some disappointment, and some adversity to toughen him up.

Yes, God wants to bless us, but we must learn to handle those blessings. Even if it doesn't feel like it right now, know that God is paying attention to you. He is out in front of you, going before you, preparing future blessings for you, and He has not forgotten about you, not even for a moment. He is attentive to you, and when the time is right, He will deliver you from your trials.

## Truth 6: God Wants to Give You Peace

"The LORD lift up His countenance upon you,
And give you peace." (Numbers 6:26)

As we consider the fact that the Lord wants to bless us, keep us, and smile on us, it should give us personal peace. When we consider that God is both gracious and attentive to us, a deep contentment should settle over our hearts. This is how Paul could write words like these:

> Don't worry about anything; instead, pray about everything. Tell God what you need, and thank him for all he has done. Then you will experience God's peace, which exceeds anything we can understand. His peace will guard your hearts and minds as you live in Christ Jesus. (Philippians 4:6-7, NLT)

Remember, Paul wrote these words in *prison*. These weren't the words of a madman, but a man who was at peace, a man fully convinced that God was in control of the details of his life. And Paul practiced what he preached, for when he and Silas were beaten severely and thrown into prison at midnight, they sang praises to God.[13]

What if they had been executed instead of released? No problem! God would keep and deliver them safely to heaven. And if they were freed, which they were, they would faithfully serve the Lord until He was done with them. Paul summed it all up by writing, "For to me, to live is Christ, and to die is gain."[14]

## Take It to the Bank!

"So they shall put My name on the children of Israel, and I will bless them." (Numbers 6:22-27)

As He wrapped up this blessing, God was saying to the priests, "You have spiritual oversight over the people. And I want you to remember to pronounce this blessing on My people over and over. I will live up to it in their lives! Don't make excuses for Me, don't soft sell this or be afraid that you're going to put expectations upon Me that I won't be able to fulfill. I will do this, so tell them!"

For the same reason, my reader, I'm telling you these things today. God has told me to tell you that He will bless you, He will keep you, He will smile on you, He will be gracious to you, He will be attentive to you, and He will give you His peace.

You can take that to the bank.

But remember, this series of promises is only for the child of God. The nonbeliever cannot claim these things. They have no right or portion in this, because blessing is really only for the believer.

There's a reason for that. The only reason we can enjoy such blessings is because Christ took the curse that belonged to us! Galatians 3:13 tells us that "Christ has redeemed us from the curse of the law, having become a curse for us (for it is written, 'Cursed is everyone who hangs on a tree')."

Jesus was cursed so you could be blessed.

Jesus died so you could live.

Jesus was forsaken that you might be forgiven.

So, the choice is yours. Do you want to experience this blessing in your life? Then you will, because it's already yours. It's like finding out you have a whole lot more in your bank account than you realized. So make a withdraw instead of going through withdrawals! Remember, God is blessing you today, smiling on you, listening to you, being gracious to you, and giving you peace.

Or, you can choose a curse.

I don't mean anything mystical by that, and I'm not speaking of any so-called "generational curse" here. I simply mean that if you do not choose His blessings, you will remain outside the circle of His blessings, facing the full penalty and repercussions of your own sins.

The choice is entirely yours.

Choose wisely, my friend!

chapter two
# Joshua's Story, Part 1:
# It's All in How You Look at Things

"For by thee I have run through a troop; and by my God have I leaped over a wall." —Psalm 18:29, KJV

**a**nd the LORD spoke to Moses, saying, "Send men to spy out the land of Canaan, which I am giving to the children of Israel; from each tribe of their fathers you shall send a man, every one a leader among them."

So Moses sent them from the Wilderness of Paran according to the command of the LORD, all of them men who were heads of the children of Israel. . . .

Then Moses sent them to spy out the land of Canaan, and said to them, "Go up this way into the South, and go up to the mountains, and see what the land is like: whether the people who dwell in it are strong or weak, few or many; whether the land they dwell in is good or bad; whether the cities they inhabit are like camps or strongholds; whether the land is rich or poor; and whether there are forests there or not. Be of good courage. And bring some of the fruit of the land." Now the time was the season of the first ripe grapes.

So they went up and spied out the land from the Wilderness of Zin as far as Rehob, near the entrance of Hamath. . . . Then they came to the Valley of Eshcol, and there cut down a branch with one cluster of grapes; they carried it between two of them on a pole. They also brought some of the pomegranates and figs. . . . And they returned from spying out the land after forty days.

Now they departed and came back to Moses and Aaron and all the congregation of the children of Israel in the Wilderness of Paran, at Kadesh; they brought back word to them and to all the congregation, and showed them the fruit of the land. Then they told him, and said: "We went to the land where you sent us. It truly flows with milk and honey, and this is its fruit. Nevertheless the people who dwell in the land are strong; the cities are fortified and very large; moreover we saw the descendants of Anak there. The Amalekites dwell in the land of the South; the Hittites, the Jebusites, and the Amorites dwell in the mountains; and the Canaanites dwell by the sea and along the banks of the Jordan."

Then Caleb quieted the people before Moses, and said, "Let us go up at once and take possession, for we are well able to overcome it."

But the men who had gone up with him said, "We are not able to go up against the people, for they are stronger than we." And they gave the children of Israel a bad report of the land which they had spied out, saying, "The land through which we have gone as spies is a land that devours its inhabitants, and all the people whom we saw in it are men of great stature. There we saw the giants . . . and we were like grasshoppers in our own sight, and so we were in their sight." (Numbers 13:1-3; 17-21; 23-33)

Some time ago, I read an article in *USA Today* about how people view or see God. The article was entitled "View of God can predict Values and Politics."

The survey, conducted by Baylor University, identified four viewpoints of God—or, as they put it, "four Gods." Baylor researchers determined the "four Gods" breakdown by analyzing questions about God's personality and engagement. The survey asked respondents to agree or disagree with any of ten descriptions of their personal understanding of what God is like, including phrases such as "angered by my sins" or "removed from worldly affairs."

The respondents could check off sixteen adjectives they believed describe God, including words such as absolute, wrathful, forgiving, friendly, or distant.

## Four Gods?

Here are the so-called "four Gods" the Baylor researchers came up with:

### 1. The Authoritarian God

This God seems ticked off most of the time. He is angry at humanity's sins, and stays very engaged in both world affairs and the life of every creature. He is ready to throw the thunderbolt of judgment down on the unfaithful or ungodly. Those who call themselves "fundamentalist" or "evangelical" (say the researchers) would subscribe to this view.

### 2. The Benevolent God

This God is still in the business of setting absolute standards for mankind, as detailed in the Bible. But those who identify with this group, drawn primarily from mainline Protestants, Catholics, and Jews, see a forgiving God, more like the father who embraces his repentant prodigal son in the Bible. They're inclined (68.1 percent of them) to say caring for the sick and needy ranks highest on the list of what it means to be a good person.

### 3. The Critical God

This God has a judgmental eye on the world, but He's not going to intervene, either to punish or to comfort. Those who identified themselves with this point of view are less likely to go to church, and are significantly less likely to draw absolute moral lines on hot-button issues such as abortion or gay marriage.

### 4. The Distant God

Followers of this God see a cosmic force that launched the world, then left it spinning on its own.

The problem I have with the definitions of God espoused by the groups listed above is that they're *all* wrong. Am I expected to choose between these four views of God—Authoritarian, Benevolent, Critical, or Distant? Which one do you believe in? None of these are working for me. I propose a fifth category.

## 5. The Biblical God

Yes, He is angry at humanity's sins, as those who believe in the Authoritarian God say. But He is not ready to throw thunderbolts at our every misstep, or we would have all been fried eons ago! He is also kind and full of mercy, as those who believe in the so-called Benevolent God say. He cares about the sick and needy in the world, and in His wisdom and love, He certainly intervenes in the lives of men and women—contrary to what those who believe in the Critical God claim. He is not an impersonal "cosmic force," as proponents of the Distant God would claim. He not only has a personality, He is the very fountainhead of personality.

In our last chapter we considered what God is like—what characterizes Him. We saw that He is both just and loving, exercising judgment as well as mercy. He loves to bless us, keep us, smile on us, listen to us, protect us, and give us peace.

How we view God is important, because it will determine how we view life as well. It will affect you in every important choice you make, including who you marry, how you live, and how you will vote.

There is really no area of your life that will not be impacted by how you view God. Take crises and problems, for instance. If you have a big God you will have small problems. If your problems seem huge and overwhelming, then you have a small God.

Obviously, some problems are very serious—in fact, really big! But how big are they in comparison with Almighty God? He is much, much bigger. It's all in how you look at things.

# A Ticket to the Wilderness

Many of us have heard the Biblical account of how the Israelites ended up wandering in the wilderness for forty years. In this chapter, we're going to find out why. (And no, it wasn't because men were in charge and refused to ask for directions!)

From their first step out of Egypt en transit to the Promised Land, the Israelites had the Ultimate GPS system. God Himself led them by day and protected them by night.

The Lord's plan for His people was a quick trek from the slavery of Egypt into the freedom and bounty of Canaan—a land God had prepared for them, flowing with milk and honey. But right out of the gate the Israelites began to murmur and complain.

I heard the story of a man who decided to join a monastery, where he took a vow of silence. More specifically, he was allowed to speak two words a year. So after the first year of complete silence, he came before the abbot of the monastery and said, "Bed's hard!"

The second year went by, and in his second two-word interview with the abbot he said, "Food's cold!" After the third year of silence, he said, "I quit!"

The priest in charge responded, "Well, it's no wonder! All you've done since you came here is complain!"

And that's all some people do . . . complain, complain, complain. Israel, like a sprinter bursting out of the starting gates, began complaining almost *immediately*. For years and years, decades and decades, the captive nation had cried for someone to deliver them. Seeing their cruel bondage and hearing their cries, God sent them Moses as a deliverer. So how did they respond to this chosen savior? For the most part, they opposed him. *Hey, who died and made you king?* (Who made you a prince and ruler over us?)[15]

Then, even after they had miraculously crossed through the Red Sea on dry ground and God had wiped out their enemies, they turned on Moses (and the Lord) yet again.

Their version of GPS was God Himself, appearing as a pillar of cloud by day and a pillar of fire by night. All they had to do was follow Him—to move when He moved, and to stop when He stopped. In the meantime, God graciously fed His people with a supernatural substance called manna. (Someone told me that the Hebrew is *"Krisp-Kremo." But I have my doubts about that.*)

Coming with the sweet morning dew, the manna was waiting for them every morning. All they had to do was walk out through their tent doors and begin picking it up in baskets. The Bible describes it as a wafer with a sweet, nutty flavor—and it fulfilled their every nutritious need. The psalmist said:

> They ate the food of angels!
> God gave them all they could hold.
> (Psalm 78:25, NLT)

But they soon grew bored with God's provision for them. They had tried all of Moses' recipes—manna muffins, manna sandwiches, manna-cotti. They said, "We remember the good old days back in Egypt. We had meat given to us free each and every day! We want meat again!" So God told Moses He was going to answer their prayer—and give them so much meat it would be coming out of their ears.

And sure enough, one day it began to rain meat! You've heard of it raining cats and dogs? This time it rained birds! Quail came dropping out of the sky, and as Israel began to gorge on raw meat, they brought a curse down on themselves. Commenting on this incident, Scripture says:

> They soon forgot His works;
> They did not wait for His counsel,
> But lusted exceedingly in the wilderness,
> And tested God in the desert.
>
> And He gave them their request,
> But sent leanness into their soul.
> (Psalm 106:13-15)

Be careful what you pray or wish for . . . you might get it! One Bible paraphrase renders Psalm 106:15 like this: *"He gave them exactly what they asked for—but along with it they got an empty heart."*[16]

I don't know about you, but I'm glad God has *not* seen fit to answer all my prayers with a "yes." Sometimes I shudder to think about some of the things I've told God I wanted or needed in years gone by. I thought I knew what would be best for me in those days, and sometimes I missed it by a mile. God knew so much better, and He wisely only gave me those things that were best for me.

There is a lot said in this story about how we are to approach the Lord in prayer. Some would tell us that we must demand of God what we want, name-it-and-claim-it, blab-it-and-grab-it . . . whatever.

Here's my bottom line on the whole issue: I would never presume to think that I know what I truly need. That is why Jesus taught us to pray *"Your* kingdom come, *Your* will be done." So we can certainly pray for whatever it is we think we want or need, but add these words— "Lord, if this is somehow outside of Your will, overrule it! Your kingdom come."

Why would I do this? Because I might be praying for the wrong thing at the wrong time, or even the right thing at the wrong time, and God alone knows what is best for me. He loves me—enough to die for me! If God says "no" to you, believe me, you wouldn't want yes! He says no to your request for your own good. He is protecting you from yourself. And God's plan for us is infinitely better than we could ever plan for ourselves. Paul describes this as the good, acceptable, and perfect will of God (see Romans 12:2).

So instead of being satisfied with God's provision, Israel griped and complained, whining and moaning at the doors of their tents. As a result, God answered their prayer just the way they prayed it, and "sent leanness to their souls."

As a pastor for over thirty years now, I have seen what happens when people take what God has blessed them with for granted. A wife tires of her husband . . . who happens to be a loving, hard-working man. Sure he has his flaws and shortcomings, and he's not particularly flashy, but he is a good provider and tries to be a good companion. But she has her eye on some other guy, or wants to be "free" again.

Her pastor and all her Christian friends tell her to stay in the marriage and appreciate her hubby. She disregards all of them, the Bible, and everything else. The Lord even puts obstacles in her path and seeks to stop her. Still she persists.

Eventually the Lord says, in so many words, "Is this what you want? Is this what you're determined to have at all costs? All right, here it is!"

At first she is elated, but then a month or two pass, and the novelty wears off. The New Mr. Right begins to look like Mr. I'm-Not-So-Sure, and she begins to have second thoughts. Her husband, however, may feel so betrayed he doesn't want to reconcile.

So what did this woman end up with? She got the desires of her heart, but God sent leanness to her soul.

Don't for a moment take any of the blessings God has poured out in your life for granted—your husband or wife, children, career, health, church, or friends. Don't ever find yourself saying, "I'm tired of this manna, and I want something else." Be careful! God may give you what you want, and you won't like it one bit.

This is also true of a person who is looking back at his or her old life, "BC," Before Christ. The devil whispers, "Remember the good old days in the world, the parties, the pleasures, the fun?" He never seems to bring up the misery, emptiness, and guilt, does he? A few random table scraps have been magnified to a royal feast in your imagination.

If you go back, if you turn away from Christ, let me warn you: All those things that you thought were so sweet and tasty will turn to ashes and bitterness in your mouth. The apostle Peter describes this unhappy return to the world in graphic terms:

And when people escape from the wickedness of the world by knowing our Lord and Savior Jesus Christ and then get tangled up and enslaved by sin again, they are worse off than before. It would be better if they had never known the way to righteousness than to know it and then reject the command they were given to live a holy life. They prove the truth of this proverb: "A dog returns to its vomit." And another says, "A washed pig returns to the mud." (2 Peter 2:20-22, NLT)

Solomon wrote: "The backslider in heart will be filled with his own ways, but a good man will be satisfied from above."[17] Being filled from now on with your own ways, cut off from the satisfaction that can only come from heaven, is a definition of hell-on-earth.

## Majority and Minority Reports

You would think the Israelites would have learned their lesson with the quail. Not so. In fact, their relationship with God was about to take a sharp turn for the worse. And it was a turn they would regret for many, many years.

The Israelites had now come to the brink of the Promised Land and were ready to enter. As a first step, God commanded them to send in twelve spies to check things out and bring back a report. And everything went downhill from there.

After exploring the land for forty days, the men returned to Moses, Aaron, and the whole community of Israel at Kadesh in the wilderness of Paran. They reported to the whole community what they had seen and showed them the fruit they had taken from the land. This was their report to Moses: "We entered the land you sent us to explore, and it is indeed a bountiful country—a land flowing with milk and honey. Here is the kind of fruit it produces. But the people living there are powerful, and their towns are large and fortified. We even saw giants there, the descendants of Anak! The Amalekites live in the Negev, and the Hittites, Jebusites, and Amorites live in the hill country.

The Canaanites live along the coast of the Mediterranean Sea and along the Jordan Valley."

But Caleb tried to quiet the people as they stood before Moses. "Let's go at once to take the land," he said. "We can certainly conquer it!"

But the other men who had explored the land with him disagreed. "We can't go up against them! They are stronger than we are!" So they spread this bad report about the land among the Israelites: "The land we traveled through and explored will devour anyone who goes to live there. All the people we saw were huge. We even saw giants there, the descendants of Anak. Next to them we felt like grasshoppers, and that's what they thought, too!"

Then the whole community began weeping aloud, and they cried all night. Their voices rose in a great chorus of protest against Moses and Aaron. "If only we had died in Egypt, or even here in the wilderness!" they complained. (Numbers 13:25-14:2, NLT)

As many times as I have read this story, it still amazes me. Twelve spies were sent in, ten brought an evil report, two brought a good one. They all saw the same thing, but they reacted differently—each according to the way he saw God.

*First, there was the majority report.* These men did not see God for who He is; all they could see were the obstacles. Their eyes were filled with roadblocks, challenges, giants, and defeat. The very idea of entering the Promised Land terrified them, and their wide-eyed, melodramatic report created a near riot. *"The land we traveled through and explored will devour anyone who goes to live there!"* What a way to describe God's provision for their lives and plans for their destiny.

*Next came the minority report.* Two of the spies sent into the land saw God for who He was. Yes, they also saw the obstacles and challenges, but because they kept God in their view, the obstacles looked like opportunities. They could already foresee the great victories Israel would enjoy as they moved into the land under God's protection.

Joshua and Caleb, two faithful men, represented the minority view. And though they reasoned and pleaded with the people, they were shouted down. It really all comes down to how you look at things, doesn't it? There will always be people who have no vision, no faith, and no interest in change.

I heard the story of an American shoe company that sent a salesman to a foreign country. He had hardly arrived before he cabled for money to come home. His reason? "No one here wears shoes!" The company brought him back and sent another salesman over.

Soon a cable arrived from this second salesman: "The market is absolutely unlimited," he exulted. *"No one here has shoes!"* Again, it's all how you look at things. It's not that Joshua and Caleb were "positive thinkers" or glossing over real problems with a Pollyanna glaze. They were simply men who had faith in God and trusted His plan completely. God would never lead them into a land without a plan to protect and provide for them!

## Mountains along the Way

We may feel our faith isn't strong enough to see miracles and move mountains in our lives. Some well-meaning friends may tell us we need "more faith" or "greater faith." But this is backwards thinking. It's not so much great faith in God that's required, as it is *faith in a great God.*

From the very beginning of my ministry, I have had people tell me to turn back, that we "couldn't do" what we felt the Lord had called us to do as we sought to take steps of faith.

When I began preaching, people told me, "You're not qualified. You're way too young." I took comfort, however, from Paul's words to Timothy: "Let no one despise your youth, but be an example to the believers in word, in conduct, in love, in spirit, in faith, in purity."[18]

After our fellowship of young people outgrew the building we were meeting in, we felt God had raised up a church, and that we needed to separate ourselves from the larger body and create our own church home.

I was told, "If you leave this facility, your group will completely fall apart!" Obviously, it didn't. We continued to grow and experience God's blessings.

When we began our evangelistic crusades, the naysayers all told us, "This will never work! It's an outmoded model. Large crusades will die with Billy Graham." (By the way, a young Billy Graham was told that large evangelistic crusades would die with Billy Sunday!) Yet in spite of the predictions of doom, we had overflow crowds and broke the attendance record at the Pacific Amphitheatre.

Outgrowing that venue, we wanted to move our crusades to Angel Stadium in Anaheim. Again, "the experts" told us that the stadium was much too big, that not many people would come, and that we would be embarrassed.

When we filled the stadium, people said, "Well, this is a Southern California thing. It won't work outside of L.A." Then we went to Oregon and Washington State, filling stadiums there. "It's a West Coast thing," people said.

Then we went to Philadelphia—about as far culturally from Southern California as you can get. When our crusade succeeded there, the response was, "Well, it's a West Coast/East Coast thing; it would never work in the South."

Wrong again. The Lord blessed our meetings in Georgia and North Carolina. The response of our critics? "It's a U.S. phenomenon. Only in America!" Then we went to Australia and New Zealand. And finally people began to say, "This must be a *God* thing."

None of this would have happened if we had listened to "the majority report" and not taken steps of faith.

The twelve spies were blown away by the sheer immensity of things in the new Promised Land. Texas-sized grapes. Texas-sized cities with Texas-sized walls. Not to mention Texas-sized warriors walking the walls of those cities. The opponents were large, but two of the spies thought the opportunities were even larger.

So what kept them from entering the Promised Land? And what keeps us from entering the Land of Promises? Once again, it comes down to how you look at things.

# What Keeps Us from the Promised Land?

What kept the Israelites out of God's land of promise?

## 1. They focused their attention on the obstacles instead of the objective.

"But the people living there are powerful, and their towns are large and fortified. We even saw giants there, the descendants of Anak! The Amalekites live in the Negev, and the Hittites, Jebusites, and Amorites live in the hill country. The Canaanites live along the coast of the Mediterranean Sea and along the Jordan Valley." (Numbers 13:28-29, NLT)

*Powerful people . . . fortified towns . . . giants . . . Amalekites . . . Hittites . . . Jebusites . . . Amorites . . . Canaanites.* (Lions and tigers and bears, oh my!) The majority report was a string of one obstacle after another.

When you fix your attention on the obstacles rather than the objective, fear will always eclipse your faith. The objective—the reason the spies were sent into the land in the first place—was to get a strategy to conquer the land, not to determine if they could do it. God had already told them they could do it!

Obstacles are the frightening things you see when you take your eyes off the objective. The Israelites were not looking at their problems in the light of God, but at God in the light of their problems.

## 2. They allowed themselves to be gripped with fear.

Their voices rose in a great chorus of protest against Moses and Aaron. "If only we had died in Egypt, or even here in the wilderness!" they complained. "Why is the LORD taking us to this country only to have us die in battle? Our wives and our little ones will be carried off as plunder! Wouldn't it be better for us to return to Egypt?" Then they plotted among themselves, "Let's choose a new leader and go back to Egypt!" (Numbers 14:2-4, NLT)

Fear stirred them into a tizzy. Wailing, moaning, weeping, whining. It wasn't a pretty picture. The fact is, trust and worry cannot coexist; when one comes in, the other goes out. In effect, they cancel each other out. When you trust you do not worry, and when you worry you do not trust.

Allowing themselves to be carried along on a wave of panic, the Israelites had talked themselves into going back to Egypt, back into bondage. Some Christians today aren't much different. A little discomfort, a few trials, a couple of dry days, and they're ready to retreat.

God will not force you into His blessing. When Gideon was putting together his army, he said to his recruits, "Anyone who trembles with fear may turn back and leave Mount Gilead."[19] In other words, General Gideon told the troops, *"Whoever is fearful and afraid, let him go home to Mommy!"* And Scripture tells us that 22,000 men took advantage of the dishonorable discharge and took to their heels.

The Christian life isn't a cakewalk, it's a conflict. It's not a playground, but a battleground. You can live in fear and unbelief and wander in the futility of your own self-imposed wilderness, or you can enter into all God has for you. It comes down to this: Do you have a big or small God?

## 3. God didn't want them to run from giants, but attack them!

Joshua and Caleb reminded Israel that the Promised Land was everything God had told them it would be—a land flowing with milk and honey (not to mention grapes the size of oranges).

> "Do not rebel against the LORD, and don't be afraid of the people of the land. They are only helpless prey to us! They have no protection, but the LORD is with us! Don't be afraid of them!" (Numbers 14:9, NLT)

These two guys were ready to strap on the armor! *"Let's go get 'em! They don't have a chance against us. They're sitting ducks. They're as good as finished!"*

All of us have giants we face in life.

You might be facing a giant of fear as you read these words. Something has frightened you and continues to frighten you, robbing you of both peace and a good night's sleep. Every time you think of that thing (which is more often than you would like), you feel it grip you by the throat, and it seems as though it will never go away. You've become paranoid, constantly worried, and even crippled by this fear. That, my friend, is a giant.

It might be a giant of some kind of sinful habit you're struggling with. A certain area of your life is weak, and you fall into this same sin over and over again. You have victory for a few weeks—perhaps even a month—then it has you again. It could be pride, envy, gluttony, pornography . . . the list goes on and on.

In a related way, you may be facing a giant of addiction. You have tried to overcome this addiction again and again, but you have failed. It has now become a towering monster in your life, something that taunts you day in and day out.

You might be a facing a giant of personal threat. Someone keeps slandering you—or they have a lawsuit out against you. Perhaps someone has actually threatened to kill you or harm your family.

On the other hand, the giant in your life might be a heartbreaking situation that just seems to go on and on . . . an unsaved husband . . . a prodigal child . . . a crushing financial situation . . . an ongoing health concern. A giant is anything that seeks to control, hurt, torment, or destroy you.

So what do you do? *Force your giant into the light of day, and go on the attack.*

Let's say it's the giant of addiction—alcohol, drugs, pornography, overeating . . . whatever it might be. First, recognize you have a problem. Stop rationalizing and excusing it. Realize you *cannot* defeat it in your own strength. Then call on God and pray for His power. Gather some godly brothers or sisters around you and pray until you have a plan. Don't let this thing keep taunting you and mocking you. Attack it!

We see this principle of attacking giants in the life of David. The entire army of Israel was paralyzed by fear as the Philistine giant Goliath prowled the battle line between the two armed camps, taunting Israel and daring them to fight. David, hardly more than a shepherd boy at the time, was on an errand for his father and happened upon this scene. The young man's blood boiled when he heard the nine-foot-tall freak belching out threats and blasphemies against God. Without hesitation, he volunteered to face off against Goliath, *mano a mano*.

But it really wasn't a one-on-one contest, and David knew it. Far from it! The God of Israel was with him, so what did it matter if there was a whole army of nine-foot, six-toed giants? David knew this was a spiritual battle that had to be won with spiritual weapons. So he prayed, and Scripture says that he *ran* out to the battle line to meet Goliath—and brought the giant down with a single stone.

You and I must do the same. Rather than cowering before those lumbering giants in your life, *attack* them. In God's strength and enabling, draw lines, make yourself accountable to others, and stay away from people or situations where you know you might be hammered with excessive temptation. Don't let that giant back in your life again.

Or let's say it's the giant concern in your heart regarding an unsaved loved one. The weeks and months go by, and that family member of friend seems as hardened to spiritual things as ever. Remember, the battle belongs to the Lord. *Attack*. Get your Christian friends together and pray about this. Commit it to the Lord each day, each hour if necessary. Then wait on Him, avoiding the temptation to force the situation and try to "help God out."

Again, don't look at God in the light of your giant. Look at your giant in the light of God!

Paul uses the wilderness wanderings of the Israelites as an allegory of the Christian life—an encouragement and a warning for last-day believers, like you and me. Like the Israelites, we were delivered from bondage. Theirs was a bondage under Pharaoh to slavery, ours was a bondage under Satan to sin.

Moses came and delivered them, as Christ did for us. God's plan for them was to enter a Promised Land—a land of blessing and yes, conflict. It was full of both serious challenges and magnificent rewards.

There is a direct correlation to our lives here. We can choose to follow Jesus Christ as Savior and Lord and embrace this life one hundred percent—even in the face of difficulties, temptations, and towering giants. (But there will also be blessings galore!) Or we can turn back from that exciting, challenging life and live in a self-imposed wilderness of struggle and halfheartedness. The choice is indeed ours.

Are you in a wilderness right now? Do you find yourself always complaining about practically everything? Have you been taking your salvation for granted? Have you been thinking about going back to your old life?

Please don't even consider that—your loss would be unimaginable! So how can you change your outlook? Start with the rebellion of the Israelites and their refusal to trust God and move on into the land of His provision. Then fast-forward forty years. The wilderness wanderings are over, Moses has passed away, and only two men remain from that whole generation: Joshua and Caleb. They're both getting up in years now, but they are clear-eyed and ready to tackle whatever awaits them. Listen to the strength in Caleb's voice!

> "Now, as you can see, the LORD has kept me alive and well as he promised. . . . Today I am eighty-five years old. I am as strong now as I was when Moses sent me on that journey, and I can still travel and fight as well as I could then. So give me the hill country that the LORD promised me. You will remember that as scouts we found the descendants of Anak living there in great, walled towns. But if the LORD is with me, I will drive them out of the land, just as the LORD said." (Joshua 14:10-14, NLT)

Wow! There's no way this guy is ready for a rocking chair and shuffleboard. He's telling Joshua, *"Let me at those giants. With God going before me, I'll mow 'em down."*

What kept Caleb going all those years? How did he keep his focus when so many did not? What is the secret of spiritual longevity?

Look back at Joshua 14:8. Reflecting on that fateful day when the spies returned from the Promised Land, he said, "My brothers who went with me frightened the people from entering the Promised Land. For my part, *I wholeheartedly followed the LORD my God"(NLT)*.

Wholeheartedly following God like Caleb means you give one hundred percent to God. So many want to get all of God's gifts and blessings, but give so little of themselves. Caleb's strength never weakened. He kept God as the first love in his life, and grew in strength through the years.

It's all in how you look at things. How do you see God? Little or big? This will determine the course your life will take. If you see Him for who He is, you will long to know and walk with Him. If you see Him for who He is, you will see this world for what it is . . . empty, pathetic, and on its way to destruction.

On the other hand, when you are only giving the Christian life your bare minimum, and your love for Jesus is not burning brightly, this world and its temporary pleasures will look more and more appealing. When that happens, you, too, will take your manna for granted and try to live in the past.

Sure, the Promised Land had obstacles and giant problems.

But Israel served a big God and so do we! The Christian life will always have its share of obstacles, challenges, and even a giant or two, but if we are *following the Lord completely,* we will have our priorities straight. We will see those obstacles as opportunities. No matter how large your problem, Your God is more than equal to the task.

It's all in how you look at things!

## chapter three
# Joshua's Story, Part 2: Overcoming or Overcome?

"For every child of God defeats this evil world, and we achieve this victory through our faith." —1 John 5:4, NLT

h ave you ever had one of those days when you were on an absolute roll in your spiritual life? God was blessing and using you in such a powerful way. You could tangibly see your steps were being ordered by the Lord.

Then, suddenly, you just blew it big time. You fell so hard you couldn't believe you had done it. You certainly didn't see it coming. In effect, you snatched defeat out of the jaws of victory.

*Why does that happen?* The answer to this question is found here in the book of Joshua.

The book of Joshua is the book of new beginnings for the people of God. The wilderness wandering of forty years had finally come to an end. It was time to enter in. Though challenging and exciting, this wasn't going to be easy. In fact, it was shaping up to be a full-blown war with the Canaanites, the inhabitants of the land.

We might ask, why is such a place given in the Word of God to record the military victories (and sometimes defeats) of the Israeli army in the conquest of Canaan? Why are we given detailed accounts of armed conflicts where blood was shed?

Because we, too, are at war.

It's not a war of flesh and blood, but a spiritual battle. It started on the day of your conversion and will rage until the day you go to heaven. You will be tempted, harassed, hassled, and attacked.

Simply put, Satan does not want you to follow Jesus Christ.

Thankfully, God knows our breaking point and won't give us more than we can handle. It's really not a choice of fighting or not fighting. It's a choice of victory or defeat . . . winning or losing . . . advancing or retreating . . . staying in the wilderness or entering the Promised Land.

In the Christian life, you are either an overcomer or you are overcome. He brought us out that He might bring us in!

> "We were slaves of Pharaoh in Egypt, and the Lord brought us out of Egypt with a mighty hand; and the Lord showed signs and wonders before our eyes, great and severe, against Egypt, Pharaoh, and all his household. Then He brought us out from there, that He might bring us in, to give us the land of which He swore to our fathers."
> (Deuteronomy 6:21-23)

As we saw in the last chapter, when the people came to Kadesh Barnea, Joshua and Caleb said, "Let's go up now and possess it, for the Lord is with us!" That's faith! But the people said, "No way! We're not able!" That's unbelief, and it cost an entire generation the opportunity to experience God's provision and rest. Instead, they wandered through a desolate wilderness for forty years.

## Surrounded

Unbelief says, "Let's stay back where it's safe." Faith says, "Let's go forward to where God is working!" The apostle John put it like this: "For whatever is born of God overcomes the world. And this is the victory that has overcome the world—our faith. Who is he who overcomes the world, but he who believes that Jesus is the Son of God?" (1 John 5:4-5).

Sometimes, however, we can feel a bit overwhelmed in this spiritual battle. I read a story from the Korean War that illustrated the kind of attitude we should cultivate in our daily warfare with the evil one. As enemy forces advanced, Baker Company was cut off from the rest of the regiment.

For several hours no word was heard, even though headquarters repeatedly tried to communicate with the missing unit.

Finally the command center received a faint signal. Straining to hear each word, a corpsman asked, "Baker Company, do you read me?"

"This is Baker Company."

"What is your situation?"

"The enemy is to the east of us, the enemy is to the west of us, the enemy is to the south of us, and the enemy is to the north of us." Then, after a brief pause, the sergeant from Baker Company said, "And we're not going to let them escape this time!"

Maybe you feel like that embattled military unit sometimes. Everywhere you look, it seems like the enemy is at work, wrecking havoc in the lives of countless people and still finding time to attack, tempt, and generally harass you.

Why is that? Because Jesus Christ is coming back! Even if some liberal theologians don't believe it, the devil knows all too well that Jesus is returning to earth soon. That's good news for us—and an incentive to share our faith and live holy lives. For the evil one, it's an incentive to attack our faith and try to make us stumble and fall. He wants to take as many down with him as possible.

We need to wake up to the reality of all of this, because the devil is never too busy to rock the cradle of a sleepy saint. Paul writes, "Do this, knowing the time, that now it is high time to awake out of sleep; for now our salvation is nearer than when we first believed. The night is far spent, the day is at hand. Therefore let us cast off the works of darkness, and let us put on the armor of light" (Romans 13:11-12).

We are at war, and the sooner we recognize that fact, the better off we'll be. God had deeded the Promised Land to the children of Israel, but they still had to enter in and *possess* what was rightfully theirs.

The same is true for us. There is no power apart from Jesus Christ that you have to submit to, no addiction that needs to control your life, and no lifestyle you cannot break free from. He whom the Son sets free is free indeed.

## Entering In

The book of Joshua, besides being accurate history of Israel conquering the Promised Land, is also a beautiful picture of warfare and victory in the Christian life. The previous four books in the Bible—Exodus, Leviticus, Numbers, and Deuteronomy—feature Moses as a symbol of the Law. Israel's wilderness years picture our needless wanderings when we don't obey God.

But Joshua pictures Jesus bringing us into a new land. The city-by-city battle with the Canaanite kings in this book has a great deal to say about the spiritual battles in which we're all engaged day by day. Commenting on all the Israelites went through, the apostle Paul wrote these words to the church at Corinth:

> These things happened to them as examples and were written down as warnings for us, on whom the fulfillment of the ages has come. So, if you think you are standing firm, be careful that you don't fall! (1 Corinthians 10:11-12, NIV)

Let's set the scene. Forty years have passed since that fateful day when Israel turned back in unbelief, refusing to enter the Promised Land. All of those original doubters who refused to trust God have passed away, and the wilderness wanderings are finally at an end.

The time had come, and God told Joshua to lead the people into the land He had prepared for them. Reminding them to obey the Word of God and to be courageous, the Lord promised that every place the sole of their foot touched was theirs to possess.

There was only one problem with crossing over into Canaan. It was the small matter of the entire nation crossing the Jordan River . . . at flood stage.

From earliest memories, the Israelites had heard about their parents crossing the Red Sea. But that was forty years ago! Now it was time for the Lord to show His power to a new generation. And once again, the Lord showed His mightiness, causing the river to dry up when the foot of the first priest who led the way stepped over the bank.

On the other side stood the ominous city, Jericho, with its massive, towering walls and thousands of armed inhabitants. It could have been incredibly intimidating to realize that this huge fortress city was to be their first military objective.

God understands the way we see things. The psalmist tells us, "For He Himself knows our frame; He is mindful that we are but dust."[20] Bearing that in mind, He prepares us for those seemingly overwhelming challenges we encounter in life. And that's what He did for Israel.

The first thing He did was to block a rushing, overflowing river at the moment when the nation needed to cross. That ought to have put some courage into every heart!

By the way, that's another good reason to make sure you meet with the Lord every morning, spending time in His Word and in prayer. You and I have no idea what the day before us will bring. We might find ourselves facing one of the greatest crisis moments in our lives—or one of the most wide-open opportunities we've ever experienced. The Lord wants to prepare us for those moments, giving us direction and filling us with His Spirit. And He will . . . if we are faithful to seek Him and meet with Him.

But He wasn't done preparing General Joshua's heart for battle. Within sight of Jericho's great walls, a mysterious visitor showed up at Joshua's campsite.

> When Joshua was near the town of Jericho, he looked up and saw a man standing in front of him with sword in hand. Joshua went up to him and demanded, "Are you friend or foe?"
>
> "Neither one," he replied. "I am the commander of the LORD's army."

At this, Joshua fell with his face to the ground in reverence. "I am at your command," Joshua said. "What do you want your servant to do?"

The commander of the LORD's army replied, "Take off your sandals, for the place where you are standing is holy." And Joshua did as he was told. (Joshua 5:13-15, NLT)

Joshua asks, "Are you friend or foe?" (Please say friend!) This commander was the Lord Himself! He was saying, in effect, "Joshua, I didn't come to take sides . . . I came to take over!"

Moses experienced the presence of the Lord in a burning bush at a turning point in His life. This was Joshua's moment, but this face-to-face encounter with God was completely different from Moses'. God came to Joshua in a way He could understand. Joshua was a soldier, so that's how the Lord appeared to him.

This reminds us that God makes Himself known to each generation—and He's not bound by how He appeared to the last generation. Our children can't live off of our faith or descriptions of our past experiences. We can teach them what we have learned, but they need their own encounter. God gave that to Israel. He was leading them a step at a time, and the challenges would grow with intensity.

## Strange Battle Plans

So the nation of Israel crossed the Jordan in the midst of a miracle, and their leader had a personal encounter with God and a promise of heaven's might in upcoming battles.

All of this was preparing them for the mighty city of Jericho. The only way this city was coming down was by the power of God. So the Lord gave Joshua the battle plan. . . .

*Throw up massive ladders on the walls, scale them, and attack!*

*Cut off food supplies and starve the inhabitants out.*

*Shoot arrows over the walls.*

No, none of the above. God had a more novel plan.

Now the gates of Jericho were tightly shut because the people were afraid of the Israelites. No one was allowed to go out or in. But the Lord said to Joshua, "I have given you Jericho, its king, and all its stromg warriors. You and your fighting men should march around the town once a day for six days. Seven priests will walk ahead of the Ark, each carrying a ram's horn. On the seventh day you are to march around the town seven times, with the priests blowing the horns. When you hear the priests give one long blast on the rams' horns, have all the people shout as loud as they can. Then the walls of the town will collapse, and the people can charge straight into the town." (Joshua 6:1-5, NLT)

Does it ever seem to you like God is just having a little fun at our expense? Of course, that's not the case, but it does seem that He is always coming up with all sorts of unusual and diverse ways to accomplish His purposes. And why does He do that?

So we will stay dependent on Him.

What if the angel of the Lord had visited Joshua and given him a basic straight-up battle plan for conquering Jericho? Joshua could have said, "Thanks, Lord. That's what I thought. I'll check in with You after it's all over."

No, one reason God gives us fresh strategies and unusual methods is so that we will simply place ourselves entirely in His care and keeping and say, "Lord, that blows my mind. I would have never thought of that. I have no idea what to do next—I'm just going to follow You step by step."

Whether it's Joshua with trumpets or Gideon with torches and pitchers or David with the "sound of marching feet in the tops of the balsam trees," God loves to use weakness to show His strength, and though it might at times seem random, it never is. Pardon the expression, but there is a method to the madness. It's really not madness at all, but God's way of keeping us looking to Him.

Do you want a classic example? Recall how God healed Naaman, the mighty Syrian general. This famous, decorated soldier had leprosy and heard of a prophet in Israel.

When he approached Elisha's residence, however, loaded with gifts and goodies, the prophet barely gave him the time of day. He said, "Go, dunk yourself seven times in the Jordan."

Why this unusual and humbling prescription? Because Naaman was a proud man, and God wanted him to strip off his armor and his finery and all he normally hid behind and expose himself for what he was: a leper . . . a diseased man who was helpless to change his condition. [21]

It's the same reason God wants us to confess our sin. It's not, *"Lord I'm already a good person, please make a little bit better."* Not that, but, *"O Lord, I'm a helpless sinner! Save me, for I have no other hope!"*

Consider the various ways Jesus healed people. He healed with a word. He healed with a shout. He healed with two touches. He spat on some dirt and made mud. You see this pattern throughout Scripture; God will often do His work in ways that seem unusual—even upside down.

*Do you want success? Don't seek it, but seek the Lord instead.*

"But seek first the kingdom of God and His righteousness, and all these things shall be added to you." (Matthew 6:33)

*You want to be happy? First learn to be sad!*

"Blessed are those who mourn, for they shall be comforted." (Matthew 5:4) [Literally, "Happy are the unhappy!"]

*You want to be great? Learn to be a servant of others.*

"Whoever wants to be first must take last place and be the servant of everyone else." (Mark 9:35, NLT)

So the Lord revealed the plan to Joshua on how Jericho would fall. March around it each day in total silence, and on the seventh day do it seven times—and then shout for all you're worth! Each day, the whole Israelite nation got into formation and quietly marched around that massive city.

Each day may have been more difficult than the last as they saw the immensity of this challenge. Those walls—how thick and high and imposing they must have seemed.

We all have Jerichos in life, problems that loom large and make our spirit tremble within us. What is the Lord seeking to accomplish in such times? Sometimes He just wants us to see how impossible the situation is apart from Him. He will march us around and around it, driving home the point that we cannot handle this in our own strength or wisdom.

For many of us, the greatest difficulty is simply coming to that place where we finally admit the whole thing is simply too big for us to tackle. *The walls are too high . . . the obstacles are too great . . . the enemy is too strong . . . the situation is too complex . . . and I'm too weak to lift a finger. If this Jericho is going to fall somehow, it is God and God alone who must bring it about.*

It was British preacher Alan Redpath who used to say, "When you get to the end of yourself, you get to the beginning of God." And that is so true. Is that where you are right now? You've been marching around your Jericho—that incurable illness, that unsolvable problem, that unsaved spouse, that failing business, that prodigal child. You think about your future and it feels like your wheels are spinning in the sand, and you don't know what to do. It's your Jericho, and God is the only one who can help you overcome it.

Just remember that His ways probably won't line up with yours.

## The Day of Reckoning

The inhabitants of Jericho were very wicked people. They used their children as prostitutes for their false gods or even sacrificed them on pagan altars. They were into every kind of idolatry, sin, and gross perversion. In His mercy, God had given them plenty of time to repent before their day of reckoning.

The reputation of Israel and Israel's mighty God had certainly preceded them. They may not have had Fox News or CNN in those days, but word got around. Most of Canaan would have heard the stories about the ten plagues, the parting of the Red Sea, and the destruction of Egypt's army, the military super-power of the day. "And you say those Israelites are on their way . . . *where?*" They certainly could have seen the handwriting on the wall and made their peace with God, but they didn't.

God patiently endured the evil of the Canaanites from the time of Abraham to Moses, a period of over four hundred years. From the Exodus to the crossing of the Jordan was yet another forty years in Israel's history. *And the Canaanites knew what was going on!* Every miracle and wonder was known, right up to the parting of the Jordan so the entire nation could walk through without even getting their sandals wet.

Do you think the Canaanites didn't hear about the manna, the water from the rock, the cloud by day and the pillar of fire by night? They'd heard. They knew. But they resisted turning to God to the bitter end. They didn't so much as lift a finger to believe, but in fact opposed Israel.

Why did God mandate that Joshua and the army utterly destroy Jericho? Because the Lord knew that living in proximity to these Canaanites would pollute and corrupt His people. The spiritual principle we can apply from this is that God will not tolerate compromise with sin in our lives!

After six days of silent marching, the day of battle finally arrived. On this seventh day, in obedience to God's explicit instructions, the people marched around the city seven times—followed by a mighty shout! Immediately, the walls of the city collapsed, and Israel's soldiers charged in to take care of business.

What a glorious story this is. Truly, one of the greatest stories ever told. But as striking as this historical account may be, what follows in the very next chapter interests me even more. We read in amazement how Israel goes from the lofty heights of victory to the lowest dregs of defeat.

# A Stunning Failure

The Bible is a brutally honest book. If our hero does the right thing, we have the full account to read and celebrate. If our hero turns out to be a zero or a villain, however, the Bible doesn't varnish it. The pages of Scripture are the only true "no spin zone." After taking down Jericho, the rest of Canaan's land was going to be a cakewalk. Yet chapter 7 opens with an ominous word.

> But Israel violated the instructions about the things set apart for the Lord. A man named Achan had stolen some of these dedicated things, so the Lord was very angry with the Israelites. (Joshua 7:1, NLT)

It had been God's plan for Israel to roll from one victory to another, overtaking their enemies in Canaan. Instead, they suffered a crushing, humiliating defeat at a little place called Ai.

*Victory unto victory.* That is God's desire for His sons and daughters. We need not fail in the Christian life if we don't want to. Defeat may happen in the life of a believer, but it doesn't have to. Yes, there will be opposition and attacks from the enemy as we march forward in obedience to God's will. Those who are making a difference for God's kingdom can count on gaining the attention of the dark side. Anyone who determines to be content with nothing less than God's best has a target on his or her back. Why? Because they are a threat!

Here's how Israel failed so quickly after one of her greatest victories.

> Joshua sent some of his men from Jericho to spy out the town of Ai, east of Bethel, near Beth-aven. When they returned, they told Joshua, "There's no need for all of us to go up there; it won't take more than two or three thousand men to attack Ai. Since there are so few of them, don't make all our people struggle to go up there."

So approximately 3,000 warriors were sent, but they were soundly defeated. The men of Ai chased the Israelites from the town gate as far as the quarries, and they killed about thirty-six who were retreating down the slope. The Israelites were paralyzed with fear at this turn of events, and their courage melted away. (Joshua 7:2-5, NLT)

So why did they fall? And for that matter, why do *we* fall?

## #1 Reason for Falling: Self-confidence

Ai was only a small city compared to Jericho, which now lay in smoldering ruins. They could do this one in their sleep! They wouldn't even need the whole Israeli army, just a few thousand men. Now, this argument was based on the supposition that *Israel* had captured Jericho. Actually, all they had done was march around its walls and shout. God had given them that victory!

Sometimes you face your greatest dangers after you have won a battle. As we will see later in this book, it was after his spectacular success on Mount Carmel that the great prophet Elijah panicked and ran away in fear. Andrew Bonar said, "Let us be as watchful after the victory as before the battle."

Remember Simon Peter's words in the upper room?

"You will all fall away," Jesus told them, "for it is written: 'I will strike the shepherd, and the sheep will be scattered.' But after I have risen, I will go ahead of you into Galilee."

Peter declared, "Even if all fall away, I will not."

"I tell you the truth," Jesus answered, "today—yes, tonight—before the rooster crows twice you yourself will disown me three times."

But Peter insisted emphatically, "Even if I have to die with you, I will never disown you." And all the others said the same. (Mark 14:27-31, NIV)

Peter heard the Lord's warning, but he couldn't believe *he* would fall. Other people might stumble, other people might turn timid, but not *him*. The big fisherman had no idea what spiritual danger he was in.

Pride, the Bible warns us, goes before a fall. Self-confidence is at the core of many sins that people commit. We tell ourselves, *I can handle this. . . . I'll know when to stop. . . . I would NEVER become an alcoholic . . . or adulterer . . . or embezzler . . . or pornography addict.*

It's like when you're at a dinner party and at the end of the meal someone orders a big dessert with four forks. If I don't take the first bite, I'm okay. But once I've taken it, I'm like a shark who smells blood in the water!

We demonstrate dangerous self-confidence when we imagine we can do what we want, when we want, with whom or against whom we want, and not suffer any repercussions. No one is above the law—especially God's law. So if you hear of someone stumbling into sin, don't be arrogant and condemning. *"How could they be so stupid! I would never do anything like that."*

Maybe . . . and then again, maybe not. Listen to the warning of Scripture:

> Dear brothers and sisters, if another believer is overcome by some sin, you who are godly should gently and humbly help that person back onto the right path. And be careful not to fall into the same temptation yourself.
> (Galatians 6:1, NLT)

## #2 Reason for Falling: Neglect of Prayer

It's clear that Joshua did not go to the Lord for a fresh battle plan for Ai. Flushed with the victory at Jericho, he thought Ai would be a walk in the park. Instead, it was a Waterloo.

Here's something to remember: If you pray in a time of victory, you will never have to plead in time of defeat. Thinking back to Simon Peter, he went from boasting that he would never deny the Lord during the last supper, to the Garden of Gethsemane, where he was told to watch and pray but took a nap instead.

Then, when the guards came to arrest Jesus, Peter woke up with a start and started swinging his sword . . . just before taking to his heels and running away. He was boasting when he should have been humbling himself, sleeping when he should have been praying, and fighting when he should have been trusting.

So how did Joshua respond to the disaster at Ai? His first response was to blame the whole thing on God!

> Then Joshua cried out, "Oh, Sovereign LORD, why did you bring us across the Jordan River if you are going to let the Amorites kill us? If only we had been content to stay on the other side! Lord, what can I say now that Israel has fled from its enemies? For when the Canaanites and all the other people living in the land hear about it, they will surround us and wipe our name off the face of the earth." (Joshua 7:7-9, NLT)

He said *what?* "If only we had been content to stay on the other side"? After all God had done for him and Israel? How quickly we forget the blessings of God.

I love the Lord's response.

> But the LORD said to Joshua, "Get up! Why are you lying on your face like this? Israel has sinned and broken my covenant! They have stolen some of the things that I commanded must be set apart for me. And they have not only stolen them but have lied about it and hidden the things among their own belongings." (Joshua 7:10-11, NLT)

The Lord is essentially saying, "Stop already! You guys brought this on yourselves! It's time to take action!" How often we disobey God, and then when we reap the consequences we blame Him for our troubles. That brings us to the third reason for defeat at Ai.

## #3 Reason for Falling: Disobedience

Someone in the camp had directly disobeyed God's solemn command. One man named Achan had stolen property which belonged to God. Ordinarily the soldiers shared the spoils of war, but in this case, God specified that everything—people, houses, animals, goods—was to be utterly destroyed. There would be plenty of goodies for the Israelites in the future, but in this particular conquest, God told them all of the bling belonged to Him! It was a small request considering the fact that He gave them the victory to begin with.

This brings up a very important point. The Bible tells us that we, too, belong to God—life, career, family, body, health, possessions, and future. It is the Lord's! The Bible says "You are not your own; you were bought at a price."[22] Yet so often we forget that, and neglect God.

Is it too much for us to dedicate time each day to pray and read His Word? It's God who gives us each and every twenty-four hour day—our every breath is in His hand. Is it too much for us to remember the Lord in our giving of finances? Scripture tells us we rob God when we fail to give! (More about that later.)

It's interesting—and very sobering—to note that the sin of one man had an impact on the whole congregation. It's still that way. Sometimes I hear people complain about the church, or why they do this or that. Let me ask you a question. *What if your church was just like you?* What if everyone attended as often as you do? Would the church be empty or full? What if everyone worshipped as you do in song? Would your church be full of praise and singing, or would it be silent? What if everyone shared the gospel as faithfully as you do? Would your community be reached for Christ? What if everyone studied their Bible like you do? Would you have a biblically literate or illiterate church?

You affect the church—whether you want to believe that or not. And no individual Christian can go his or her own way and commit sin without affecting the whole body. As Alan Redpath used to say, "No child of God can grown cold in his spiritual life, without lowering the temperature of everyone else around him." The victory of the church as a whole depends on the victory of each individual member. That is why we should want to build up and help one another, rather than berating each other and tearing each other down.

Achan's sin affected his family, his people, and his nation. One man outside of the will of God is a menace to everyone else! Look at the prophet Jonah. God had sent him to Nineveh to warn the city of impending judgment. But instead of heeding the clear call of God, he disobeyed and caught a ship headed in the opposite direction. As a result, God sent a storm to shake that ship and everyone on board . . . until Jonah repented.

Are you outside of the will of God and dragging others down? What kind of spiritual influence do you have on those you rub shoulders with every day? You *are* being watched, and you *do* have influence, whether you realize it or not.

If find yourself getting continually knocked down spiritually, maybe it's because there is unconfessed sin in your life. The Bible says, "If I regard [hold onto or cling to] iniquity in my heart, the Lord will not hear me" (Psalm 66:18, kjv).

Speaking of the forbidden items Achan had stolen, the Lord told Joshua, "You will never defeat your enemies until you remove these things from among you" (Joshua 7:13, nlt).

How did the sin of Achan go down? Pretty much the way all sin goes down! Joshua told Achan to come clean, and the man confessed: "Indeed I have sinned against the Lord God of Israel, and this is what I have done: When I saw among the spoils a beautiful Babylonian garment, two hundred shekels of silver, and a wedge of gold weighing fifty shekels, I coveted them and took them. And there they are, hidden in the earth in the midst of my tent, with the silver under it" (Joshua 7:20-21).

This was a sin from the get-go, and Achan knew it.

## Three Steps to Disaster
### The first step: he saw

Most temptation starts right here. This is the way merchants get you into their stores. I read an article in *USA Today* about how retailers encourage customers to shop in their stores. Apparently, it's not only with displays and mannequins wearing the latest styles.

At the SonyStyle store they have developed a signature fragrance of vanilla and mandarin orange that wafts down on shoppers, relaxing them and encouraging them to hang around.

Other retailers use different scents in different departments. Bloomingdales uses baby powder in the baby store, suntan lotion in bathing suit area, and, well, you get the idea. We are drawn toward temptation through our senses.

It's not always the first look that gets us into trouble, but the second! Jesus mentioned this in the Sermon on the Mount when He warned of lustful looking. You can't help seeing what you see, but you can help following that mental pathway toward lust. I like the old quote from Martin Luther. He said that he couldn't stop the birds flying over his head, but he could stop them from building a nest in his hair!

## The second step: he coveted

Coveting is a powerful and underestimated sin that can cripple you spiritually, and ultimately destroy you. It must not be downplayed or left unchecked. Think of some of the people in the Bible who threw everything away—their life and possibly their eternity—because of greed and covetousness. Judas betrayed Jesus for thirty pieces of silver. And as we just read, Achan's unrestrained act of coveting led to the death of at least thirty-six of his fellow soldiers, his own life, and the lives of his wife and children. *For a new robe and some money?* What a price!

Paul said it so well to his young associate, Timothy:

> But godliness with contentment is great gain. For we brought nothing into the world, and we can take nothing out of it. But if we have food and clothing, we will be content with that. People who want to get rich fall into temptation and a trap and into many foolish and harmful desires that plunge men into ruin and destruction. For the love of money is a root of all kinds of evil. Some people, eager for money, have wandered from the faith and pierced themselves with many griefs. (1 Timothy 6:6-10, NIV)

It's not a sin to want to be successful in business and make a good living. But when you become obsessed with it . . . when you are willing to do whatever it takes to get there . . . when it becomes the most important thing in life to you, coveting has become idolatry.[23]

## The third step: he took

Achan thought that, somehow, he could get away with breaking God's command. Didn't he understand that the God who could split the Jordan River for His people to walk across, the God who pushed down the mighty walls of Jericho with the flick of His little finger, would see what he was doing? Did he really think he would somehow pull one over on God and slip by?

The Lord once asked Jeremiah, "Can anyone hide himself in secret places, so I shall not see him? . . . Do I not fill heaven and earth?"[24]

Scripture warns, "Your sin will find you out!"[25] By the way, that statement was issued to God's people, not lost people.

We all have our Jericho's and Ai's. Our victories and defeats. Are you facing a Jericho right now? Put it in God's hands. Ask Him for His wisdom and direction, and wait on Him to show you what to do. His methods may surprise you, but the end result will be infinitely better than you could have planned for yourself.

Are you recovering from an Ai? Get up off the ground, face up to the sin, own up to the disobedience, receive God's forgiveness, and move on to the next battle.

God's grace will get you moving, and God's power will push down your walls.

## chapter four

# Gideon's Story:
# When a Little Is a Lot

"Go in this strength that is yours. . . .
Haven't I just sent you?" —Judges 6:14, THE MESSAGE

Sometimes it seems like our nation's language has been turned upside down. If you were to take someone from the late 1950s, put them in a time machine, and drop them off in the middle of today's culture, they would be hopelessly confused.

Just look at the expressions we use. Certain slang expressions have not stood the test of time; words like "groovy" and "far out" have seen their day. But other expressions going back to the fifties—I'm thinking of the word "cool"—are still in use today.

Then there's the word "hot," as in "that's hot." What's strange is that something can be both cool and hot at the same time!

If something is good we say "that's bad!" We'll look at a hot (cool?) car and say, "How fast will that *bad boy* go?" That's because bad is good. Then if something is *really* good we say, "That's killer!"

So good is bad, and really good is killer, and really, really good is *sick*. (You need to be or know a teenager to get this one, and it will most likely be out of date by the time this book is in print!)

Now in the old days, if someone was doing drugs, sexually loose, and partying, you would say "that's bad." And that's exactly what we meant. The person who was principled, moral, and didn't use drugs was "good." We said what we meant.

But how do you say it now? Is he so good he's bad, or is he so bad he's good? Is he so hot he's cool, or is he so cool he's hot?

Hollywood, through music, movies, and TV, has only reinforced this confusing state of affairs. Does God have anything to say about this confusion of terms? Yes, He does. In the book of Isaiah, the Lord says,

> Woe to those who call evil good
> and good evil,
> who put darkness for light
> and light for darkness,
> who put bitter for sweet
> and sweet for bitter.
>
> Woe to those who are wise in their own eyes
> and clever in their own sight. (Isaiah 5:20-21, NIV)

The cultural confusion and anything-goes attitude of this twenty-first century is certainly nothing new. In fact, in the book of Judges, the seventh book of the Bible, the state of things in the nation of Israel was really turned upside down.

One verse in that book summarizes the whole situation:

> In those days there was no king in Israel; everyone did what was right in his own eyes. (Judges 17:6)

God raised up thirteen judges—twelve men and one woman—to guide His people through this chaotic, roller-coaster period of Israel's history. When we think of "judges" here, we must not think of Supreme Court judges in black robes. These were more like Wyatt Earp or one of the lawmen of the Wild West. The country needed someone to keep a semblance of law and order in the land . . . but even so, these were wild and crazy times in Israel.

## A Sad Contrast

As the book of Judges begins, Joshua has died. What a sad contrast between Judges and Joshua! Though they are right next to each other in the Bible, they are worlds apart. Joshua is primarily the record of the adventures and exploits of Israel as they obeyed God and entered into the Promised Land.

Joshua is the story of conquest, while Judges is a book primarily about defeat. Joshua is a book of faith, while Judges is a book of unbelief and disobedience. Joshua is a book about people uniting around one man to lead them, and Judges is about everyone doing what was right in their own eyes.

It was the year 1256 BC, and approximately 200 years had passed since Joshua had led the Israelites on their famous march around the walls of Jericho. By God's power, Israel saw those walls implode, and they went on to conquer many of the inhabitants of Canaan, including the Amorites, Hittites, Ammonites, and Jebusites. There were many battles over many years, but they didn't finish the job. They failed to drive all the Canaanites out, and lived to regret it.

There's a parallel here to our lives as Christians. We may commit ourselves to the Lord and give Him the master key to multiple doors. At the same time, however, we keep a couple of closets for ourselves . . . dark, hidden, and locked. We may think our secret sins are closed off from the rest of our lives, but it's only a matter of time before the contents of those hidden closets begin to haunt us.

As Judges chapter 6 opens, we see the tribes of Israel living under the cruel dominion of the Midianites. This occupation of the nation was God's discipline in their lives as a direct result of their disobedience. Israel did evil in the sight of the Lord, so He handed them over to the Midianites (Judges 6:1).

The Midianites were the first in history to domesticate the camel, giving them a huge military advantage. Have you ever checked out a camel? They are big, fast, ugly, and can go days without water. And they spit, too! Can you imagine seeing your enemies swooping down on you riding these things—by the thousands? It would be terrifying.

Every year at the time of harvest, these Midianites would invade Israel like a plague of locusts and appropriate all the crops for themselves. Nearly in despair, Israel finally remembered they had an Almighty God and called on Him to deliver them.

In answer to those prayers, the Lord Himself showed up, picking out a candidate for national hero and deliverer.

God's choice for the job of champion would have surprised everyone. It certainly surprised the candidate himself!

## "Who . . . Me?"

As our story begins, we find a man named Gideon trying to prepare the little bit of wheat that he'd managed to glean, hiding behind the walls of a small winepress. Hardly a picture of heroism and courage. Like the rest of Israel, he was hungry, hurting, and humiliated. But in Gideon's story we will discover the kind of qualities God is looking for in the person He will use for His glory.

> Now the Angel of the LORD came and sat under the terebinth tree which was in Ophrah, which belonged to Joash the Abiezrite, while his son Gideon threshed wheat in the winepress, in order to hide it from the Midianites. And the Angel of the LORD appeared to him, and said to him, "The LORD is with you, you mighty man of valor!"

> Gideon said to Him, "O my lord, if the LORD is with us, why then has all this happened to us? And where are all His miracles which our fathers told us about, saying, 'Did not the LORD bring us up from Egypt?' But now the LORD has forsaken us and delivered us into the hands of the Midianites."

> Then the LORD turned to him and said, "Go in this might of yours, and you shall save Israel from the hand of the Midianites. Have I not sent you?" (Judges 6:11-14)

Gideon's response is interesting. He's essentially saying, "If God has chosen me, why is everything going wrong and where are all the miracles we heard about in days gone by?"

I heard the story of a mother who was telling some Bible stories to her little girl, talking about Creation, the parting of the Red Sea, and the miracles in the lives of men like Moses, Joshua, and Daniel. The little girl turned to her mom and said, "Mommy, you know, God was much more exciting back then!"

That's how Gideon felt. He'd heard about the good old days, but where was God now? It's a valid question. In Gideon's case, it could have been answered with a rebuke. *You're suffering because you and your people have forgotten Me and worshipped false gods!* But the Lord was very patient with Gideon.

Verse 14 says that "the LORD turned to him." It could better be translated "The Lord looked at him." After making eye contact, He simply said, "Go in this might of yours, and you shall save Israel from the hand of the Midianites. Have I not sent you?"

God could have taken the time to rehearse the whole situation going back to Joshua's day, but He's basically telling Gideon, "Let's not get into that right now. It would take too long. Here's how I plan to resolve the crisis you're in right now."

This wasn't a time to question or criticize, but to take some action! There is a time to pray and there is a time to move. I've always been a pretty practical guy. I tire of long, drawn out meetings where people philosophize about this and that. I am more the kind of person who wants to identify the problem, come up with the best solution, and get after it!

Gideon, however, wasn't seeing this at all.

He replied to the Lord, "O my Lord, how can I save Israel? Indeed my clan is the weakest in Manasseh, and I am the least in my father's house." (Judges 6:15)

In other words, "I'm the runt of the litter!" It reminds me of another young man in Scripture who was the youngest and least in his father's house. That young man's name was David, and God had big plans for him.

## God Uses People Who Are Humble

This gives hope to all the people out there who are not extraordinary, but ordinary. They weren't the best students, or class president, or homecoming queen. They weren't the first chosen for the team, but the last. They didn't make the cover of *People's* "World's Most Beautiful People." They don't have great natural talents.

God can do amazing things through people like this—people who see their shortcomings, but also the greatness of God.

When Jesus called Simon Peter, Peter responded, "Depart from me, for I am a sinful man!" *Don't waste your time on me Lord; I'll only let You down!* But Jesus saw Peter for who he would become, not just who he was.

God tells Gideon He will do the work through him. "And the LORD said to him, 'Surely I will be with you, and you shall defeat the Midianites as one man' " (Judges 6:16).

"Who am I?" Gideon asks in verse 15.

"That's not the issue!" the Lord says in verse 16. "It doesn't matter who *you* are, for I have said *I* will be with you!"

"If God be for us, who can be against us?" the Scripture asks.[26] Notice how God addressed Gideon: "The LORD is with you, you mighty man of valor!" I love this! Another translation says, "Mighty hero, the LORD is with you!"[27]

It could almost sound like mockery. In Joshua, the expression refers to brave soldiers marching into the heat of battle. It would be like going up to a scrawny little guy and saying, "Hey, you buffed-out bodybuilder!"

If there was anything Gideon was *not* at that moment, it was a mighty hero. He was more like a pathetic zero! God sees us for who we can become, not who we are.

We see a lump of clay, God sees a beautiful sculpture.

We see a blank canvas, God sees a Rembrandt.

We see a lump of coal, God sees a sparkling diamond.

We see a Gideon hiding in a winepress, God sees a mighty man.

We see a vacillating, unsure Simon, God sees a rock like Peter.

We see a persecuting Saul of Tarsus, God sees a mighty apostle Paul.

We see failure, God sees potential.

By the way, some of the greatest successes come from failure. The doorway of success is often entered through the hallway of failure. Sometimes failure functions simply as a process of elimination. Thomas Edison once said, "Many of life's failures are people who did not realize how close they were to success when they gave up."

Gideon felt unworthy of such a privilege and responsibility and needed some reassurance from the Lord, so God gave him a miracle.

Gideon replied, "If you are truly going to help me, show me a sign to prove that it is really the LORD speaking to me. Don't go away until I come back and bring my offering to you."

He answered, "I will stay here until you return."

Gideon hurried home. He cooked a young goat, and with a basket of flour he baked some bread without yeast. Then, carrying the meat in a basket and the broth in a pot, he brought them out and presented them to the angel, who was under the great tree.

The angel of God said to him, "Place the meat and the unleavened bread on this rock, and pour the broth over it." And Gideon did as he was told. Then the angel of the LORD touched the meat and bread with the tip of the staff in his hand, and fire flamed up from the rock and consumed all he had brought. And the angel of the LORD disappeared. (Judges 6:17-21, NLT)

God had done His part, and now it was time for Gideon to get started. God usually leads us one step at a time. He wants us to be faithful in the little things before He will give us more to do. Some may want to journey to faraway lands and speak to isolated people groups. That's an excellent goal. But maybe the first thing God would have you do is talk to the coworker who works beside you all day.

In the gospel of Luke, Jesus said, "Whoever can be trusted with very little can also be trusted with much, and whoever is dishonest with very little will also be dishonest with much. So if you have not been trustworthy in handling worldly wealth, who will trust you with true riches? And if you have not been trustworthy with someone else's property, who will give you property of your own?" (Luke 16:10-11, NIV).

We all would like to be used of God. But start with small things. All of our pastors at Harvest Christian Fellowship started in our Helps Ministries, including the parking lot crew, ushering, counseling, and teaching Sunday school. They proved themselves faithful in the little things before they were given greater responsibilities.

What opportunities has God set before you right now? It's interesting that when Jesus spoke about faithfulness with small things, He began with money! "And if you are untrustworthy about worldly wealth, who will trust you with the true riches of heaven?"[28]

You talk about all you want to do for God. But let me ask you this: Do you give regularly of your finances to God as He commands? If you can't be faithful in something as simple as that, why would you expect you would do more if you had more? "No," you say, "if I had more money I would give more to God." It's all relative. The fact is, if you had more money, you might spend more money and still not give! Wherever you are in life, you need to honor the Lord with your finances. God will bless you for it.

> Honor the LORD with your wealth and with the best part of everything you produce. Then he will fill your barns with grain, and your vats will overflow with good wine. (Proverbs 3:9-10, NLT)

Gideon had a test for God, but God also had a test for Gideon. His first task was to tear down the altar his father had built to Baal. The Lord told him to take the second best bull from his father's herd and barbeque it on the remains of this altar. Gideon did as God commanded.

Gideon did what the Lord commanded, but it wasn't exactly like he did it at high noon. In fact, he waited for the middle of the night. Some commentators criticize him for that, but I think it's still admirable. Sure, he did it under cover of darkness, but at least he did it! Again, I admire people who get the job done!

There are a lot of critics out there who may argue around and around about the best way to do something, and never actually accomplish anything at all. Then there are the Gideons and Simon Peters of life who fumble here and there, but still get the job done. I would rather try and fail than never try at all.

Yes, Gideon did it at night. But that was no true indication of where he would end up as a warrior and leader for the Lord. Just because someone doesn't start out with great promise, doesn't necessarily mean they won't come around in the end. We all remember the devoutly religious man Nicodemus who came to Jesus by night. This is mentioned a few times in Scripture, so it's noteworthy. He probably did that because he was afraid of what others would think.

Nicodemus was a famous man, a household name. Jesus asked, "Are you the teacher in Israel and you don't know these things?" So though he may have had a weak beginning, he had a much better ending. For instance, Judas Iscariot was a full-fledged apostle in good standing while Nicodemus was still groping his way in. Yet at the end of our Lord's ministry, Judas betrayed Jesus and went and hanged himself. But old Nicodemus stepped forward when all the disciples had forsaken the Lord and fled Him. In company with Joseph of Arimathea, they boldly approached Pilate to take and care for the body of Jesus. [29]

So you may have a feeble beginning but a strong finish. Better that than a strong beginning and no finish (because you gave up and turned back!).

Gideon tore down the altar of Baal his father had erected. When everyone discovered it the next morning, they were aghast! They called for the execution of Gideon. Instead of turning on his son, the father defends him, and seems to have his own faith rekindled.

Listen, the hardest people to reach will always be your own family. As Jesus said, "A prophet is not without honor except in his own town." Even Jesus' mother and siblings did not believe in Him till his death and resurrection!

And can you imagine being one of Jesus' siblings? He was flawless! He never sinned, was never a poor witness. Can't you just hear Mary saying, "Why can't you be more like your brother Jesus? He always does the right thing!"

"But Mom . . . Jesus is perfect!"

"I know, honey," Mary might have responded. "But you need to ask yourself the question each day, 'What would Jesus do?' "

Don't give up on your family. You don't need to preach sermons to them all day long. You need to show your faith by the way you live and the decisions you make.

Gideon, however, still had his doubts. So he laid more tests before God, including his infamous fleece before the Lord. God accommodated Gideon's doubt and unease, and confirmed His word again and again.

Finally, this reluctant "man of valor" was reassured, and relatively ready for the task at hand: to deliver Israel from the Midianites. For that, of course, he needed an army, and Gideon was able to rally 32,000 men. Not nearly enough to take on a superpower like Midian, but a good enough beginning.

And that's about the time the Lord took out His pruning shears.

> The LORD said to Gideon, "You have too many warriors with you. If I let all of you fight the Midianites, the Israelites will boast to me that they saved themselves by their own strength. Therefore, tell the people, 'Whoever is timid or afraid may leave this mountain and go home.' " So 22,000 of them went home, leaving only 10,000 who were willing to fight. (Judges 7:2-3, NLT)

Of all the upsets celebrated by military historians or sports fans, none is more stunning than the one God accomplished through Gideon. He was basically outnumbered 450 to 1, and yet Gideon's army won a crushing victory over the Midianites. It would be like a Pop Warner Team going up against the New York Giants. Or a little league team taking on the Los Angeles Angels. The Midianite army was huge!

The armies of Midian, Amalek, and the people of the
east had settled in the valley like a swarm of locusts.
Their camels were like grains of sand on the seashore—
too many to count! (Judges 7:12-13, NLT)

God wants to get the glory for the work He does. So He
will often let things stack up in such a way that there is *no way
out but Him.* There will be that insurmountable obstacle like the
Red Sea He wants us to get through. There will be the towering
walls of a Jericho He wants us to fell. There will be the frightening giant Goliaths He wants us to defeat.

But it's not us doing it for God, but God doing it through
us and sometimes for us. There is always His part and our part.

The Red Sea parted, but Israel had to march through.

The walls of Jericho fell, but Israel still had to march
around them.

The giant Goliath fell, but David still had to attack.

Peter pronounced the crippled man at the Temple gate
healed, but he still had to pull him to his feet.

Are you overwhelmed by the odds right now? There's no
way out of your situation but God! Believe it or not, that's a
good place to be.

I love the prayer of Jehoshaphat when facing huge odds as
an enemy army approached. He prayed, "O our God, will You
not judge them? For we have no power against this great multi-
tude that is coming against us; nor do we know what to do, but
our eyes are upon You" (2 Chronicles 20:12).

Literally, he prayed, *"We are looking to you for help."*

So Gideon tells the cowards to go home. Why? Because fear
is contagious. In the same way, if you're looking for life on Easy
Street with no conflict or challenge, go home! But if you want
to be used by God, and want your life to make a difference,
move forward!

Gideon was probably expecting a few to turn tail and run
for home. *But 22,000?* That was two-thirds of his army! There
was one final test now for Gideon and Israel. This was to be a
secret test.

But the LORD told Gideon, "There are still too many! Bring them down to the spring, and I will test them to determine who will go with you and who will not." When Gideon took his warriors down to the water, the LORD told him, "Divide the men into two groups. In one group put all those who cup water in their hands and lap it up with their tongues like dogs. In the other group put all those who kneel down and drink with their mouths in the stream." Only 300 of the men drank from their hands. All the others got down on their knees and drank with their mouths in the stream.

The LORD told Gideon, "With these 300 men I will rescue you and give you victory over the Midianites. Send all the others home." (Judges 7:4-7, NLT)

This test revealed the soldiers' attitude toward the enemy. One group just thought about water. They were the lappers. Basically, they forgot about the Midianites and just satisfied their thirst. They could have been easily ambushed and killed.

God said, "Send 'em home, Gideon."

Then there were the cuppers. These kneeled, bringing the water to their lips while still watching. They were alert, cautious, not letting down their guard. And there were only 300 of them in the whole bunch.

So Gideon is now down to the top three percent of the 10,000. He's down to the cream of the crop, the Delta Force, the Seals, the Green Berets, the SWAT team!

Then God gave the battle plan to Gideon. He was to divide his force into three groups, instructing them to take a burning torch covered by a clay jar in one hand, and to carry a trumpet in the other.

What kind of a battle plan was that? It was beginning to sound as strange as God's plan for taking Jericho—marching silently and then shouting!

So Gideon's elite force of Israeli warriors crept up on the vast Midianite camp without knife, sword, spear, or slingshot. They had clay jars, they had shielded torches, they had trumpets, and they had a battle plan.

Then he said to them, "Keep your eyes on me. When I come to the edge of the camp, do just as I do. As soon as I and those with me blow the rams' horns, blow your horns, too, all around the entire camp, and shout, 'For the LORD and for Gideon!' " (Judges 7:17-18, NLT)

It's so crazy it's classic. But that's just what they did. In the middle of the night, the Midianites were startled by the sudden flaring of three hundred torches, the blast of three hundred ram's horns, and the shouts of three hundred men filled with faith and adrenaline.

Utterly panicked, the enemy soldiers drew their swords and began slicing and stabbing at each other. In the end, the Midianites were utterly routed.

## Thinning Out the Ranks

So what does a story like this have to say to us today? More than we may realize.

In John chapter 6, just when Jesus seemed to be riding the crest of popular fame and acclaim, He delivered a tough sermon that perplexed and disgusted the crowds of followers.

The apostle John tells us that after that time, "many of His disciples went back and walked with Him no more" (v. 66).

Why did Jesus do this? Why did He intentionally thin out the ranks of His followers—on more than one occasion? Because He knew the hearts of those followers and hangers-on. He knew that many of them—perhaps most of them—were there to see a big show, some dramatic miracles, and maybe collect a free meal or two. Those who truly loved Him and were devoted to Him were relatively few.

That was the dynamic behind the thinning of Gideon's army. After the reluctant, the fearful, and the careless went home, only 300 remained. But with this 300, God gave to Gideon and the Israelites the victory.

God said to Gideon, "By the 300 I will save you . . ."
Why did God impose this test? He wanted to get rid of the halfhearted people, the fair-weather followers, those who had no real heart for Him. Listen, God can do more with 300 committed people than 10,000 reluctant followers!

God was and is looking for men and women who will love Him more than anyone or anything else. English evangelist John Wesley once said, "Give me a hundred men who love God with all of their hearts and fear nothing but sin, and I will move the world."

Once, when the crowds kept growing and growing, following Him everywhere, Jesus turned to them and spoke very directly.

> "If anyone comes to Me and does not hate his father and mother, wife and children, brothers and sisters, yes, and his own life also, he cannot be My disciple. And whoever does not bear his cross and come after Me cannot be My disciple." (Luke 14:26-27)

Jesus laid out the cost of discipleship to the curious, the hangers-on, the casual followers. The groupies, if you will. In describing true discipleship, Jesus said some of the most solemn and searching words that ever fell from His lips. In the course of this message, He said three times, "cannot be my disciple." In other words, these are absolute prerequisites to true discipleship. Let's look at them together.

## Hate Loved Ones?

"If anyone comes to Me and does not hate his father and mother, wife and children, brothers and sisters, yes, and his own life also, he cannot be My disciple." (Luke 14:26)
What's this all about? Christians are supposed to "hate"?

Jesus was using a form of speech that would have been very familiar to His audience. He used the oriental method of sharp contrasts, and the word "hate" is used as the opposite of "love." If there is ever a time when the highest, most noble of earthly loves comes into conflict with Christ and His cross, the call of Christ must prevail!

But why would Jesus say such things to all those people who followed Him? It was almost like He was intentionally trying to get rid of them.

In a sense, He was. At least some of them.

Jesus wanted to winnow out the casual, non-committed followers, those who had no real heart for Him. Looking back to Gideon's story, we find that God can do more with 300 alert, committed men than he can with 32,000 who are halfhearted. God is still looking for men and women who will shake their world. Men and women who will be true disciples. If you're looking for a life of ease, with no conflict or sacrifice, then the life of a disciple is not for you.

Remember, God *will* test us as Christians. Do you remember when you were in school and the teacher would make a dreaded announcement something like this? "Class, today I'm giving a pop quiz."

That rather bizarre group of diligent students with too many pens in their pockets and tape wrapped around the bridge of their glasses would actually smile with glee at such an announcement! (We used to call these people geeks and nerds; now we call them boss!)

The teacher might add, "If you've been paying attention, you have nothing to worry about!" Well, of course my stomach sank because I *hadn't* been paying attention. And needless to say, I failed many a test.

Sooner or later we have to learn the material or we will never advance. Well, God gives pop quizzes too, and he rarely, if ever, announces them ahead of time. They just come. We think we know certain truths so well. We love to tell others how to do it. And then the Lord, through a test in our lives, says, in essence, "Let's see how well you've been listening."

A true disciple will be one who is drinking in his Master's every word, marking every inflection of voice with an intense desire to apply what's been learned.

So Jesus was testing the people. Looking for real disciples. What was that first test? What did Jesus mean when He spoke about "hating" family members? He chose this analogy to show how our love for God must take preeminence over all others.

The point is, you will either have friction in your relationship with the Lord and harmony with people, or harmony in your relationship with the Lord and friction with people! Jesus warned, "Beware when all men speak well of you." You can't have it both ways! It's one or the other! Your love for others must be like hatred when laid alongside your love for God.

Are you a wholehearted follower of Jesus Christ, loving Him so passionately that all other loves in your life pale by comparison? Is there someone in your life you are putting ahead of the Lord today? It may be a person in your family that you love more than God Himself. It may be a relationship you're involved in right now. You know you are compromising God's standards and risk losing God's best for your life, but you're afraid of displeasing that someone. It may be that you've put your career ahead of the Lord, or maybe there's some other pursuit that you won't give up no matter what.

Will you become a true disciple of Jesus today, and love Him more than anyone or anything else? Will you step out from the "fickle multitudes" and "fair-weather followers" to walk with Him through the rest of your life? Will you be like one of Gideon's 300 and volunteer to join in great exploits for your Lord?

If that's your commitment today, get ready for an exciting life.

And watch those Midianites scatter.

# chapter five
## Samson's Story:
## He–Man with a She–Weakness

"Get her for me, for she looks good to me."
—Judges 14:3, NASB

ife is full of surprises.

Many are unexpected pleasures and blessings that come our way. Others are tragic and sad.

I have been greatly surprised by the way certain people's lives have turned out. I can think of people I've met through the years who seemed to have no potential whatsoever. You never expected these guys or girls to amount to much of anything. Maybe you even made fun of them in school. Then, five or ten years after graduation, you hear one of these "geeks" is the president of a multi-million-dollar software company!

Then there are those whose lives seemed to be brimming over with promise and potential. They had something special, and you just knew they would make their mark in life. Blessed with multiple talents, giftedness, and personality, they seemed to stand out from the crowd. Perhaps it was someone who was unusually gifted spiritually. And sure enough, their star began to rise, and you're thinking, "Well, at least I can say I knew them back when."

Then suddenly, seemingly without warning, the bottom seems to drop out of this individual's life. Or you watch in perplexity as The Golden Boy, The Golden Girl, are slowly sidetracked by foolish, life-marring decisions.

Stories like that are always very sad, because God has a unique, custom-designed plan for each of our lives. And when we stubbornly turn from His path to follow our own ways or the impulses of our flesh, our personal loss is incalculable.

The prophet Jeremiah tells the story of his trip to the potter's house, where he watched as the craftsman molded clay into useful vessels. On the potter's wheel, the pliable, shapable clay could be made into something both useful and beautiful.

That is a picture of our lives. We're the ones who determine if we will be flexible and moldable in God's hands. We make ourselves that way by our openness to His plans and our willingness to obey. I believe the steps of our lives are allowed by God before our conversion, and ordered by the Lord after. God knew the day you would receive Christ, and He has allowed your life experiences in order to do a unique and never-to-be-duplicated work in your life.

At this very moment, even as you read these words, you can be pliable and shapable in God's hands, or you can continually resist Him. He gives you that choice.

For instance, after all the tragedies and setbacks in young Joseph's life (read his story in Genesis 37–50), he could have adopted a victim mentality and become bitter. Instead, he chose to be *better*. After many years of watching God work through the ups and downs of his life, he could still say to his brothers, "As for you, you meant evil against me, but God meant it for good in order to bring about this present result, to preserve many people alive. So therefore, do not be afraid."[30]

Outside of the potter's house described in the book of Jeremiah[31] was a field littered with cracked, broken pots and vessels. Wreckage. Lives that could have been objects of beauty and great usefulness to God—but would not yield. These broken shards represent wasted potential.

Before us in this chapter is the story of a man who had off-the-charts potential that was largely wasted. Gifted with unbelievable physical strength, Samson had God's blessing and anointing on his life. He could have been one of the greatest leaders in the history of Israel. But instead, his life became a proverb, an example of how not to live.

When you think of Samson's life, you think *waste.* A life of squandered resources and untapped potential and ability. He threw it away because of some subtle but ultimately fatal errors in judgment. His life stands as a warning to all of us.

Time and again in Scripture, however, the streams of tragedy and hope run side by side. Samson's story also speaks of second chances . . . and the grace of God.

## The Devil in the Details

The life of Samson illustrates the ancient truth that a good beginning doesn't necessarily guarantee a good ending. That's basically what Solomon wrote: "The end of a thing is better than its beginning" (Ecclesiastes 7:8). The American poet Henry Wadsworth Longfellow said, "Great is the art of beginning, but greater is the art of ending."

When we think of Samson's tragic fall, our minds race to his encounters with Delilah. But the fact of the matter is, it was a series of smaller compromises that ultimately proved to be his undoing.

Many of us vividly remember the explosion of the space shuttle Challenger on January 28, 1986. Seven crew members died in that tragic mishap. After weeks of careful research, technicians revealed that the primary cause of the explosion was a failure of something called an "o-ring."

O-rings are rubber rings used as mechanical seals or gaskets. When an o-ring failed on Challenger's rocket booster, it allowed the super-heated gasses from the burning rocket to escape, ultimately resulting in the explosion.

It's mind-boggling to think of that shuttle—something so large, so powerful, so incredibly expensive, so carefully designed—being brought down by something as small and seemingly insignificant as an o-ring.

Samson's life was similar. We can trace a breakdown in the smaller areas of his life . . . leading to an explosion.

Some of you who read these pages are young, with tremendous potential to make a difference for God in this very dark world at this crucial time in history. Through the life of Samson, God warns you to walk with great care so that you don't repeat this mighty man's mistakes. But the story isn't just a red flag for young people. All of us need to attend to the details of our lives, seeking to walk before God with a whole heart.

## A Great Paradox

Samson's life stands as one of the greatest paradoxes in the Bible. He had such magnificent potential to do something truly great for God, and to lead his people out of the state of backsliding into which they had fallen.

Humanly speaking, Samson had superhuman qualities. Physically, there was none stronger. Mentally, he was sharp, clever, and alert.

And spiritually? He had an admirable start in life. He was one of the two men in the Old Testament whose birth and mission were foretold by angels. Of Samson it was said, "The boy is to be a Nazirite, set apart to God from birth, and he will begin the deliverance of Israel from the hands of the Philistines."[32]

He certainly *began* that job, and he may have been able to *finish* the task had he allowed that potential to reach full bloom. For this calling, he was given a special anointing of the Holy Spirit that gave him strength like no other.

These were extremely dark days in Israel's history. As the Bible describes it, everyone did what was right in his own eyes, and the Word of the Lord was scarce. The people of God had been living compromised lives and didn't want to rock the boat with their enemies, the Philistines. So as God always does when the times turn spiritually and morally dark, He raised up a deliverer. Someone to turn the light on.

As prophesied before his birth, Samson chose to live a life separated to God, taking the vow of a Nazirite. Among other things, the provisions of that vow included the following restrictions:

1. A Nazirite was to separate himself from all wine and liquor.

2. He was to avoid all contact with a dead body.

3. He was to be holy unto the Lord.

4. No razor was to ever touch his head.

When we think of Samson, we remember his long hair. In fact, his supernatural strength was symbolized by those untrimmed locks. If it was the same today—if hair still represented physical strength—some of us bald guys wouldn't get on very well!

But it wasn't his hair that gave Samson strength, it was his wholehearted commitment to God, symbolized by the hair.

From the very beginning, it was clear that God was with this young man in a special way. Scripture tells us that "he grew and the LORD blessed him, and the Spirit of the LORD began to stir him. . . ."[33]

But no sooner does this promise begin in Samson's life than he flatly disobeys God's commands and marries a Philistine woman. Clearly, this was what Scripture calls an "unequal yoke." God tells us to avoid such relationships for very good reasons. For every case where that nonbeliever has come to faith, there are probably a hundred cases of the believer being dragged down and spiritually compromised. Ignoring his parents' objections, Samson did what he wanted and married her. Why did he do that? Because she looked good. As he told his parents, "Get her for me, for she looks good to me."[34]

## Hooker, Line, and Sinker

A series of mishaps followed, resulting in the breakup of that potential marriage. In conflict after conflict, Samson used his God-given superhuman strength to achieve victory over Israel's Philistine overlords.

The troubles and trials in this young man's life should have been a divine wake-up call for him. It was an opportunity for him to learn from his mistakes and turn around before it was too late.

Instead, he went the other way.

Refusing to heed God's warnings, Samson went from the frying pan into the fire. The devil got the mighty Samson *hooker*, line, and sinker!

> One day Samson went to the Philistine town of Gaza and spent the night with a prostitute. Word soon spread that Samson was there, so the men of Gaza gathered together and waited all night at the town gates. They kept quiet during the night, saying to themselves, "When the light of morning comes, we will kill him."
>
> But Samson stayed in bed only until midnight. Then he got up, took hold of the doors of the town gate, including the two posts, and lifted them up, bar and all. He put them on his shoulders and carried them all the way to the top of the hill across from Hebron. (Judges 16:1-3, NLT)

What was a Nazirite doing in a Philistine city's red light district? Certainly no one forced him to do it. He deliberately made this choice and crossed the line. As far as he was concerned, no ambush could hurt him, no trap could hold him. So in his supreme self-confidence, he blatantly took this radical step.

Clearly he was not walking with the Lord at this point, for we read of no spiritual struggle, either before or after he headed for the land of his enemies to consort with a prostitute.

No one talks much about this first part of Samson's downfall. But in this episode with the harlot in Gaza, we discover all the seeds of his future destruction. What he sowed in Gaza with the prostitute he later reaped with the devious Delilah.

When his enemies discovered Samson was in the city, they laid plans to trap him inside the walls. Posting a guard by the house, the Philistines set up an ambush by the city gates. Studded with nails and covered with metal, these massive gates were virtually fireproof. And once locked, there was no way out of the city . . . for an ordinary man, at least.

The ambushers went to sleep, confident their nemesis could not escape. In the middle of the night Samson left the prostitute's house, put his arms around the gateposts—timbers driven deeply into the earth—and tore out the gates, posts and all, dumping them some twenty miles away!

Needless to say, no one attacked Samson that day.

But when you think about it, this display of God-given might was just another chapter in a tragic story. Samson had power without purity. Strength without self-control. For twenty years he had experienced the thrill of victory—without once tasting the agony of defeat! That should have kept him thankful to God. Instead, it produced a deadly complacency about his spiritual life.

Some may even think because God doesn't discipline or exercise His judgment immediately, that He doesn't see or doesn't care about our sins. That's a big mistake! As Paul made clear, "Don't be misled: No one makes a fool of God. What a person plants, he will harvest."[35]

Samson demonstrated he had no integrity in his life when it came to women . . . and that did not escape the notice of Satan. Having found his "in," the devil moved in for the kill. He custom-designed a delectable little dish named Delilah.

## Desperate Measures

Some time later Samson fell in love with a woman named Delilah, who lived in the valley of Sorek. The rulers of the Philistines went to her and said, "Entice Samson to tell you what makes him so strong and how he can be overpowered and tied up securely. Then each of us will give you 1,100 pieces of silver."

So Delilah said to Samson, "Please tell me what makes you so strong and what it would take to tie you up securely."

Samson replied, "If I am tied up with seven new bowstrings that have not yet been dried, I would become as weak as anyone else."

So the Philistine rulers brought Delilah seven new bow-strings, and she tied Samson up with them. She had hidden some men in one of the inner rooms of her house, and she cried out, "Samson! The Philistines have come to capture you!" But Samson snapped the bowstrings as a piece of string snaps when it is burned by a fire. So the secret of his strength was not discovered. (Judges 16:4-9, NLT)

These Philistines were desperate. Samson seemed to slaughter them for sport. On one occasion he killed thirty of them, seemingly without effort, to settle a bet. Then, finding himself surrounded, he killed a *thousand more with a mere bone he had found.* What can you do with a guy who rips lions apart and walks off with city gates on his shoulders? It was intolerable. Determined to bring Samson down, the Philistine leaders offered Delilah big bucks to find the secret of his strength.

No doubt Delilah was an attractive woman.

But what kind of bait would you expect Satan to use?

Temptation often comes in attractive packages . . . desirable, appealing, and very costly. It promises life but brings death. Is there a "Delilah" in your life now?

Once again, Samson had involved himself with the wrong person. First there was the Philistine woman, then the prostitute, and now Delilah. Samson had blatantly ignored every warning shot that God fired across his bow . . . and Satan was about to cash in on this he-man's she-weakness.

Realizing he couldn't bring this warrior down on the battle-field, Satan switched to the bedroom and found a willing victim. Did Samson ever realize the stakes of the game he was playing, toying with Philistine women? He must have thought he could just laugh it off and walk away from it all. But he was about to walk into a trap he couldn't shrug out of. (The tip-off for Samson should have been that Delilah worked at Super-Cuts!)

For temptation to do its damage, there must be a desire on our part. The apostle James wrote: "But each one is tempted when he is drawn away by his own desires and enticed.

Then, when desire has conceived, it gives birth to sin; and sin, when it is full-grown, brings forth death."[36]

In other words, for Satan to succeed, we must listen, yield, and, most importantly, desire what he offers. Our adversary will use different types of bait to tempt us. But remember, it's not the bait that constitutes sin, it's the bite!

Delilah definitely plied her seductive charm on Samson. But one thing must be noted. The lady was certainly up front with her intentions!

> So Delilah said to Samson, "Please tell me where your great strength lies, and with what you may be bound to afflict you." (Judges 16:6)

This would be the first indication that this was not a healthy relationship! Couldn't Samson have realized what was going on? Did he think it was all a big game?

Sin is so intoxicating. And it leads us to lie to ourselves. ("I can quit anytime I want to.") Samson thought he could handle it. Famous last words!

You've heard the rationalizations—and maybe even used them in times past. "I'll just go so far and then stop. Just this one time, and I'll never do it again." In response to statements like these, the Bible asks a very relevant question: "Can a man scoop fire into his lap without his clothes being burned?" (Proverbs 6:27, NIV)

Answer? Probably not, unless he's wearing asbestos.

Can you believe how blunt Delilah was? "Will you please tell me exactly how I can trap you so the Philistines can come in and capture you?"

How many wake-up calls did God give Samson? Sadly, Samson had already taken the bait. And you've got to hand it to Delilah, she was persistent! As the pretty lady kept begging and pouting and crying, Samson came closer and closer to revealing the true secret of his strength.

The story of Samson highlights some very important truths for our survival in the midst of the spiritual warfare that rages all around us.

## 1. Moral compromise always makes us vulnerable.

If Samson had not begun this sinful relationship with Delilah and the other Philistine women, he would not have found himself in this deadly situation.

Nobody falls suddenly into sin. It may look that way to an outside observer. It may even seem that way to the one who falls. But the truth is, each major compromise is preceded by a series of small compromises.

And those small compromises? They may appear to be so insignificant to you that "playing the edge" seems like no big deal.

*—What's wrong with a little soft pornography? I can handle it.*

*—Why shouldn't I go out for a few drinks with the old gang? I know when to quit.*

*—Who really cares if I fudge a little on my expense account? It's almost expected.*

*—Why shouldn't I date a nonbeliever? It's not like we're getting married.*

Is there any moral compromise in your life right now? If so, deal with it. Because someday, in some way, shape, or form, Delilah will show up on your doorstep.

And you may find yourself in a trap that has no back door.

## 2. Temptation comes in attractive packages.

The Philistines didn't go out and hire some homely woman to ensnare the Hebrew champion, they hired a fox! When sin comes, it will not come as something ugly and destructive, but rather as something desirable, seemingly good, and fulfilling.

The Bible says that the fruit of the tree in the Garden was pleasant to look upon. In other words, it looked more like a ripe, succulent peach than it did a pinecone!

### 3. Temptation comes when we choose the wrong friends.

Samson had a consistent ability to choose the wrong people to hang out with. First it was the Philistine girl that so distressed his godly parents, then the prostitute from Gaza, and finally Delilah . . . who was pure poison.

Paul nailed it when he wrote: "Do not be misled: 'Bad company corrupts good character.'"[37]

After following several false leads, Delilah turned up the heat and went in for the kill.

> Then Delilah pouted, "How can you tell me, 'I love you' when you don't share your secrets with me? You've made fun of me three times now, and you still haven't told me what makes you so strong!" She tormented him with her nagging day after day until he was sick to death of it.

> Finally, Samson shared his secret with her. "My hair has never been cut," he confessed, "for I was dedicated to God as a Nazirite from birth. If my head were shaved, my strength would leave me, and I would become as weak as anyone else."

> Delilah realized he had finally told her the truth, so she sent for the Philistine rulers. "Come back one more time," she said, "for he has finally told me his secret." So the Philistine rulers returned with the money in their hands. Delilah lulled Samson to sleep with his head in her lap, and then she called in a man to shave off the seven locks of his hair. In this way she began to bring him down, and his strength left him.

> Then she cried out, "Samson! The Philistines have come to capture you!"

When he woke up, he thought, "I will do as before and shake myself free." But he didn't realize the LORD had left him.

So the Philistines captured him and gouged out his eyes. They took him to Gaza, where he was bound with bronze chains and forced to grind grain in the prison.
(Judges 16:15-21, NLT)

What a sad story. Delilah had said to him, "If you really love me, you will do this." Now that's just about the oldest line in the book. Listen, any person who asks you to compromise your principles as a believer to prove your love *doesn't really love you.* And you would do well to get out of such a relationship as fast as you can.

*If you love me, you'll go all the way with me.*
*If you love me, cover for me! Lie for me this one time.*
That's not love at all!

What's so amazing to me is that Samson felt comfortable enough with Delilah to fall asleep in her lap! Talk about "sleeping with the enemy." And within this passage, we can find one of the saddest statements in the Bible.

*"He didn't realize the LORD had left him" (v. 20).*

He had lost his once-close connection with God, but wasn't even aware of it. This is so typical of someone trapped in sin. Everyone else sees, everyone else knows, and several brave people may even take the risk to warn that individual. But he or she responds with defensiveness, indignation, and hostility. *Everyone's against me. No one understands me. What right do they have to judge me?* And on and on it goes.

Then one day they wake up and it's too late. Life has changed forever, and there is no going back.

When Satan finally nailed God's champion, he tossed Samson aside like yesterday's garbage. The text says, "He was bound with bronze chains and forced to grind grain in the prison."[38]

And out of this last verse, we see several tragic characteristics of sin.

## Sin Blinds, Finds, and Grinds

### First, sin blinds you.

You find yourself doing completely irrational things. Insane things. I know of men with great families—loving wives and adoring children—who left it all for some stupid fling with another woman. I know of many women who have done the same, leaving devoted husbands—even their children—in some mindless quest to "find themselves."

This is insanity, and words can't even describe how deeply they will regret it one day. Ah, but that prospect of sin is so very promising at the outset. You start by fantasizing about it. *What would it be like if I did thus and so with so and so. . . .* Maybe you move from there to a little "harmless" flirting. That can easily lead to sharing intimate problems, even discussing your marital woes with that individual.

When someone questions you, you say, "Relax. We're just good friends, nothing more." Or maybe, "He really understands me," or "She really listens to me."

If you're that deep into self-justification, it's obvious that you've been blinded by sin. And if you think you can get yourself entangled and just walk away, you'd better take a page out of Samson's notebook. That's what he thought too

### Second, sin finds you.

You may very well experience a euphoric-like excitement the first time you cross the line in an extramarital relationship . . . or indulge in that sexual encounter . . . or visit that elicit Web site . . . or get away with that lie . . . or experiment with those drugs. You feel somehow above the normal constraints others face. It will be different for you, you tell yourself. You'll have your cake and eat it too. No, you won't. Your sin will find you out!

And what's that sound you hear?

*"The Philistines are upon you!"*

## Third, sin grinds you.

Satan is all about selling you an experience, but keeping quiet about the price tag. And don't kid yourself—you *will* pay a terrible price. I want to go back to a no-nonsense passage of Scripture I partially quoted earlier. Paul wrote:

> Don't be misled—you cannot mock the justice of God. You will always harvest what you plant. Those who live only to satisfy their own sinful nature will harvest decay and death from that sinful nature. But those who live to please the Spirit will harvest everlasting life from the Spirit. (Galatians 6:7-8, NLT)

The price tag for an adulterous affair includes broken marriages, betrayed trust, a damaged witness, a shattered reputation, and devastated children with deep wounds they will most likely carry for the rest of their lives.

That's a pretty steep bill. And that's without mentioning the possibility of AIDS, venereal disease, and depending on what you've done, maybe even jail time! But who cares about all that? It's all about your "needs," right?

Samson found out the hard way what a horrible, devastating thing unconfessed sin can be. But even in this mess there was hope!

Judges 16:22 says, "However, the hair of his head began to grow again after it had been shaven." This is the "life verse" for all of us folically-challenged guys (otherwise known as bald men).

Samson was now a blind slave of enemies who desperately hated him. How could life sink much lower than that? But even then, well beneath the Philistine's radar, God was working again in Samson's life . . . *as his hair began to grow back.*

This passage tells us God holds out hope to us even if we have failed. God did indeed give Samson another chance. The truth is, we're all going to have our stumbles and failures.

But here's the underlying question: How will we respond to those disappointing letdowns and setbacks? What will we learn that will enable us to "fall forward," laying hold of the forgiveness of God and avoiding that trap in the future?

If, we continue to repeat the same mistakes and excuse our sins, blaming them on circumstances, people, or whatever, we seal our own fate! And in time, we, too, will end up with a wasted life.

As Samson's hair began to grow, strength trickled back into his body. He could feel it! One night the Philistines were having a drunken feast to their vile god, Dagon. Sometime during the festivities, someone came up with the bright idea of dragging the sightless Samson out of the dungeon to make fun of him.

It turned out to be a very bad idea . . . for them.

A servant guided the now-blind champion to the foundational pillars of the temple, where the Philistines were partying away. Israel's one-time hero asked God for one final surge of strength and pushed those pillars apart, collapsing the temple and killing more Philistines in that one action than he had in his entire lifetime.

Poetic justice? Certainly that. But tragically, Samson went down with them.

We can't look at the wreckage of Samson's life without thinking about another young man who was temped sexually, but with a very different conclusion than Samson.

## A Life in Contrast

His name was Joseph, a godly young Hebrew slave serving in the household of an Egyptian official named Potiphar. Joseph was a handsome and well-built man, and Potiphar's wife laid eyes on him from the first time he entered the household. As the days went by, she pressured young Joseph to have sex with her *every single day.* This woman was more relentless than Delilah! Finally, tired of waiting, she grabbed hold of his tunic and pulled him down onto her bed.

So what did Joseph do?

He did what any reasonable person should do under such circumstances. He ran like the wind!

Though he lived hundreds of years before the Paul, Joseph did exactly what the apostle counseled young Timothy: "Run from anything that stimulates youthful lusts. Instead, pursue righteous living, faithfulness, love, and peace. Enjoy the companionship of those who call on the Lord with pure hearts" (2 Timothy 2:22, NLT).

Unlike Samson, who thought he could play with sin and not be hurt, Joseph knew his limits and simply didn't trust himself to dabble with immorality. Wisdom beyond his years!

Paul told the Corinthians: "Therefore let him who thinks he stands take heed lest he fall."[39] Joseph knew he was vulnerable, so he fled!

I'm reminded of an old Chinese proverb that says, "He who would not enter the room of sin must not sit at the door of temptation."

Fleeing sexual temptation is a no-brainer. It would be like walking across a field and coming upon a coiled rattlesnake looking at you through those glazed eyes, ready to strike. What do you do? Try to negotiate with the rattler? Reach some sort of compromise, perhaps? Do you just stand there, trying to stare it down, or even approach it to show how strong you are?

If you do, I hope your will is in order. No, if you have half a brain you back off and run as fast as you can. It is better to shun the bait than to struggle on the hook!

Flee temptation, and don't leave a forwarding address. Every temptation is an opportunity to flee to God. Are you squandering your life right now on something or someone that's destroying you from the inside out? Are you flirting with sin? Watch out!

Learn the lesson of Samson. It isn't enough to know what is right, or even to be used by God in a powerful, earth-shaking way.

*You have to finish the race.* So let's get on with it. Don't neglect the small things in your life—like those little o-rings—lest you crash and burn.

Samson may have had more muscle than Joseph, but who was stronger? The man or woman who leans heavily on the Lord will never live to regret it.

chapter six
# David's Story, Part 1:
# The Man After God's Heart

**"I have found David the son of Jesse, a man after My own heart, who will do all My will."** —Acts 13:22

**h**ave you ever felt unloved and under-appreciated? Has it ever seemed to you as though your faithful work always goes unnoticed in life? Have you ever faced a problem so large it seemed like it could never be overcome?

Then keep reading . . . because you'll find encouragement in this chapter.

The Old Testament book of 1 Samuel introduces us to David, one of the Bible's most significant people. In battle, he was fearless. In leadership, he was discerning and wise. Yet David was more than some action-movie macho-dude. He had a tender heart toward God, and was both a poet and musician.

Most significantly, he is the only man in all the Bible to be called "a man after God's own heart." And it's one thing to have someone else say that about you—maybe your pastor or your best friend or your brother-in-law. But when God Himself declares that about you . . . that's a milestone for anyone.

I have found David the son of Jesse, a man after My own heart, who will do all My will. (Acts 13:22)

David is mentioned in the New Testament more times than any other Old Testament character. When we think of David, two other names spring to mind.

David and Goliath . . . and David and Bathsheba. In many ways, those two names sum up his life. One signifies his greatest victory, the other, his most devastating defeat.

Sometimes in horse racing or politics, they talk about a "dark horse" coming from somewhere back in the pack to win the race.

The title has never fit anybody better than this young son of Jesse. No one in Israel could have imagined or expected that this shepherd boy would rise to the throne of Israel.

This was a period of history, following the era when Israel was ruled by judges, when the people began demanding a king so they could "be like the other nations." They wanted someone inspiring and noble to lead them in battle against their enemies.

So God gave them the perfect candidate. If David was the man after God's own heart, than Saul was the man after *man's* own heart. Saul had it all going. He was from a good family, tall, strikingly handsome, and in the beginning at least, modest and humble. In addition to all of that, Scripture says that "the Spirit of God came upon him in power"[40] to accomplish the tasks at hand and save the nation from its enemies.

Saul started off very well . . . but all too soon began to self-destruct. His offenses started somewhat small, then snowballed. By the time 1 Samuel 16 rolls around, Saul was already finished. He would stay on the throne for forty more years, but God had rejected him and no longer blessed his reign.

But God had another plan. God *always* has a plan. He had already selected a new man for the job and set the wheels in motion to bring David to throne of Israel. It was as though the Lord was saying, "All right, I gave you a king after your own heart, just like the other nations. You asked for him, and you got him. Now it's My turn!"

To say God's selection was a surprise would be a classic understatement. No one, not even the great prophet Samuel, saw it coming.

Why did God pick David, the youngest son of Jesse? We need to pay careful attention to this choice, for in His selection of David the Lord is showing us the kind of person He is looking for . . . the kind of person He will use in His kingdom.

And yes, God is actively looking for people to use! Never doubt it. In the book of Ezekiel the Lord said, "I looked for a man among them who would build up the wall and stand before me in the gap on behalf of the land so I would not have to destroy it, but I found none" (Ezekiel 22:30, NIV).

In years to come, the prophet Hanani told a fickle king of Judah, "The eyes of the LORD search the whole earth in order to strengthen those whose hearts are fully committed to him" (2 Chronicles 16:9, NLT).

God found in David a man who would stand in the gap, a man whose heart was fully committed to Him. Will He find a heart like that in you?

David was really just a boy at this point, but one with seemingly limitless potential. So the Lord sent the prophet Samuel to go anoint a new king of Israel.

The timing couldn't have been better for Samuel. The old prophet had slipped into a depression over the failure of Saul. He had probably come to think of the young man like a son. (His own sons were corrupt and a deep disappointment to him).

So God spoke to Samuel, told him to shake off his funk, and directed him to an obscure little village called Bethlehem.

> Now the LORD said to Samuel, "You have mourned long enough for Saul. I have rejected him as king of Israel, so fill your flask with olive oil and go to Bethlehem. Find a man named Jesse who lives there, for I have selected one of his sons to be my king."
>
> But Samuel asked, "How can I do that? If Saul hears about it, he will kill me."
>
> "Take a heifer with you," the LORD replied, "and say that you have come to make a sacrifice to the LORD. Invite Jesse to the sacrifice, and I will show you which of his sons to anoint for me." (1 Samuel 16:1-3, NLT)

So Samuel did as the LORD instructed. When he arrived at Bethlehem, the elders of the town came trembling to meet him. "What's wrong?" they asked. "Do you come in peace?"

"Yes," Samuel replied. "I have come to sacrifice to the LORD. Purify yourselves and come with me to the sacrifice." Then Samuel performed the purification rite for Jesse and his sons and invited them to sacrifice, too. (1 Samuel 16:1-5, NLT)

Interestingly, the Lord did not reveal to Samuel (at that point) who the man was to be. This is typical of the Lord. He leads us one step at a time. As much as I've wanted it at times, God rarely gives me a detailed blueprint of all that He wants me to do. More often, He just tells me to take a certain step of faithful obedience, and I am to act on it. God's way becomes plain when we start walking in it. Obedience to revealed truth guarantees guidance in matters unrevealed.

Remember the story of Philip's unexpected journey in the book of Acts? A powerful evangelist, Philip had been experiencing wide open doors and hearts in Samaria. Signs and wonders shook the city, and people were almost lining up to hear the gospel. Evil spirits were beating a path out of town, and Dr. Luke tells us that "there was great joy in that city."[41]

Right in the middle of the big Samaritan crusade, however, Philip suddenly received puzzling new marching orders.

But an angel of the Lord spoke to Philip saying, "Get up and go south to the road that descends from Jerusalem to Gaza." (This is a desert road.)[42]

*Okay,* Philip might have been thinking. *I'm in the biggest evangelistic campaign of my life and the Lord tells me leave town and head south . . . into the desert. What is this all about? Does He want me to preach to lizards?*

Actually, there is no indication Philip thought anything of the sort. He simply obeyed the word of the Lord and hit the road. The Holy Spirit didn't give him any explanation, and Philip didn't ask for one.

> So he started out, and on his way he met an Ethiopian eunuch, an important official in charge of all the treasury of Candace, queen of the Ethiopians. This man had gone to Jerusalem to worship, and on his way home was sitting in his chariot reading the book of Isaiah the prophet. The Spirit told Philip, "Go to that chariot and stay near it."
> (Acts 8:27-29, NIV)

What followed was the dramatic conversion of an important foreign official—possibly the very first African convert to Christianity. Philip had been successfully serving the Lord in a city . . . but because he obeyed God's word step by step, he had the opportunity to touch a continent!

In Samuel's case, he knew that he was supposed to go to the village of Bethlehem and crown the next king of Israel—whoever it was. So the great prophet suddenly showed up, and Scripture says, "the elders of the town trembled at his coming."[43] Why were they shaking in their sandals? A guilty conscience, maybe? Maybe it was like seeing a highway patrolman in your rearview mirror, and your heart beats a little faster. You're thinking, "What did I do?"

Bethlehem, close as it may have been to Jerusalem, was definitely off the beaten path. Years later, in the book of Micah, God would say:

> But you, Bethlehem Ephrathah,
> Though you are little among the thousands of Judah,
> Yet out of you shall come forth to Me
> The One to be Ruler in Israel. . . .
> (Micah 5:2)

This was not only David's home, but because Jesus was of the lineage of David, it would be His birthplace as well. Samuel tells the town elders that he's there to offer a sacrifice, and that he wants everyone to show up. This would give him a chance to check out Jesse's sons.

Immediately, Samuel is drawn to Eliab, the pick of the litter.

When they arrived, Samuel saw Eliab and thought, "Surely the LORD's anointed stands here before the LORD."

But the LORD said to Samuel, "Do not consider his appearance or his height, for I have rejected him. The LORD does not look at the things man looks at. Man looks at the outward appearance, but the LORD looks at the heart."

Then Jesse called Abinadab and had him pass in front of Samuel. But Samuel said, "The LORD has not chosen this one either." Jesse then had Shammah pass by, but Samuel said, "Nor has the LORD chosen this one." Jesse had seven of his sons pass before Samuel, but Samuel said to him, "The LORD has not chosen these." So he asked Jesse, "Are these all the sons you have?"

"There is still the youngest," Jesse answered, "but he is tending the sheep."

Samuel said, "Send for him; we will not sit down until he arrives."

So he sent and had him brought in. He was ruddy, with a fine appearance and handsome features.

Then the LORD said, "Rise and anoint him; he is the one."

So Samuel took the horn of oil and anointed him in the presence of his brothers, and from that day on the Spirit of the LORD came upon David in power. Samuel then went to Ramah. (1 Samuel 16:6-13, NIV)

What a fascinating story this is! Father Jesse proudly parades his seven sons before the visiting prophet. The magnificent seven!

But the Lord said, "No . . . not that one . . . not him either . . . no . . . no . . . next." So Samuel asks, "Do you have any other sons?" Take note of Jesse's reply: "There remains yet the youngest, and there he is, keeping the sheep."[44] This phrase "the youngest" doesn't just mean David was less in years than the others. It means that he was least in his father's estimation. So much so, Jesse would not have even included him had Samuel not asked if there were any others.

How sad it is when parents show favoritism to one child over another. Isaac and Rebekah both did this, with Isaac favoring Esau and Rebekah favoring Jacob. It ended up tearing their family apart.

Perhaps you felt unappreciated by your parents. They rarely expressed their affection toward you or had an affirming word for you. Or perhaps they divorced, and you never really knew their love.

Know this: Those who are rejected of men are beloved of God. You need to know that in spite of your parent's lack of love for you, you have always had a heavenly Father who deeply loves you.

David later wrote, "Though my father and mother forsake me, the Lord will receive me."[45]

Alan Redpath once wrote: "The thought of God toward you began before He even flung a star into space, then He wrote your name on His heart. It was graven in the palm of His hands before the sky was stretched out in the heavens."

So the magnificent seven have been paraded before Samuel, and to his chagrin, not one of them is God's candidate. So he asks to see this last son, the youngest, who wasn't even invited to the party.

Imagine David at that moment. He's out with the sheep in the field like any other day. Someone says, "Hey, David, they want you back at the house!"

David comes sprinting in, smelling like the sheep he had been keeping company with. He was a teen with reddish hair and a pleasant way about him. God says to the prophet, *That's My boy*. The next thing David knows, this old prophet is pouring oil on him and saying, "This is the next king of Israel!"

Those watching these proceedings probably thought Samuel was going senile! *David? King?* It was too ridiculous to contemplate. Imagine the shock, and then the jealousy, of David's brothers. Especially Eliab!

But there was no mistaking it. David was clearly God's choice, reminding us yet again that God sees things differently than we do. This brings us to the first principle about the people God uses.

## 1. God Uses Ordinary People

David was in many respects the polar opposite of King Saul. Where Saul came from a family where he was loved and doted on, David apparently came from one where he was neglected, even disliked. While Saul was the most handsome man in Israel, David was just an ordinary shepherd boy, though a good-looking one. Saul was attractive on the outside; inside he was vain, shallow, and devoid of true integrity. In contrast, though very young, David had a deep spiritual life and intense devotion to God.

But why does God seem to go out of His way to use ordinary people? A paraphrase of 1 Corinthians 1:26-28 records these words of the apostle Paul:

> Take a good look, friends, at who you were when you got called into this life. I don't see many of "the brightest and the best" among you, not many influential, not many from high-society families. Isn't it obvious that God deliberately chose men and women that the culture overlooks and exploits and abuses, chose these "nobodies" to expose the hollow pretensions of the "somebodies"?[46]

You always hear the excited buzz when some famous athlete or celebrity embraces faith in Christ (or at least appears to). We want to say to nonbelievers, "Look, we have Celebrity X on our side now!" And then we want to put them on Christian TV and rush them out into the public to represent us, disregarding the warning from Scripture that tells us to not elevate a new convert.[47] But so often that celebrity falls short and we are embarrassed.

God seems to go out of His way to choose the unexpected person. Why? "So that no man may boast before God."[48]

When the religious elite of Jerusalem encountered Peter and John after the resurrection of Jesus, they didn't know what to make of them. Weren't these men just common, uneducated fishermen? Where did all the boldness and the penetrating speech come from? Why were these men so different? Then they acknowledged that these men *had been with Jesus.*

You see, God wants the glory for what He has done and is doing. And the recruits He looks for to carry His work forward will probably look very different from the people we might have picked. Just like Samuel, we get hung up on a person's appearance. But God looks right past that into the heart.

Dwight L. Moody once had a man say to him, "Moody, the world has yet to see what God can do with and in and through the man who is wholly dedicated to Him!" Moody replied, "I want to be that man!" And God took a shoe salesman and made him one of the greatest evangelists in human history. He went from selling soles to saving souls!

## 2. God Looks for Truly Spiritual People

I'm not speaking here of some pompous "holier-than-thou" spirituality, but the real thing. The most spiritual people I have met have been very down-to-earth. I have no interest in some phony head-in-the-clouds mysticism, but rather a genuine day-by-day relationship with the living God.

Knowing and walking with God is essentially a *practical* matter, and those who really know Him will be some of the most real and touchable people you will ever meet.

Real people? We've certainly met them in the pages of this book, haven't we? Men like Jacob, Moses, and Gideon weren't cardboard cutouts or representations in a stained glass window. They put their sandals on one foot at a time like the rest of us. They were human through and through.

That's the kind of spirituality I'm talking about with David; it was practical, but it was also deeply committed to God. For insight into who David really was, one only has to read the Psalms. He had a deep hunger for God and a strong commitment to what was right.

In Psalm 57:7 (KJV), he wrote, "My heart is fixed, Oh God, my heart is fixed." That was David's heart: focused, not fickle; meditative, yet brave and courageous. In Psalm 27 he really laid out the whole purpose of his life:

> One thing I have desired of the Lord,
> That will I seek:
> That I may dwell in the house of the Lord
> All the days of my life,
> To behold the beauty of the LORD,
> And to inquire in His temple. (v. 4)

David was saying, "Wherever You are, Lord, that's where I want to be—just as close as I can get. That's the chief desire of my life."

It sounds a little like the apostle Paul, doesn't it? He, too, had that clear, singular aim and objective: "One thing I do, forgetting those things which are behind and reaching forward to those things which are ahead, I press toward the goal for the prize of the upward call of God in Christ Jesus."[49]

Mary had singleminded devotion as she sat at Jesus' feet, drinking in every word. At that point, her sister Martha did not have that singular focus, leading Jesus to say, "Martha, Martha, you are worried and troubled about *many* things. *But one thing is needed,* and Mary has chosen that good part, which will not be taken away from her."[50]

Do you have this clear focus and aim in your life? Or do you have double vision as you find yourself trying to live in two worlds? Our greatest danger in life is in permitting the urgent things—those pressing, insistent details of life—to crowd out the important.

What was this one thing that David desired?

> To behold the beauty of the LORD,
> And to inquire in His temple.

Perhaps you have felt the same way. You love being with God's people at church, and you wish you could set up camp under the nearest pew and just live there.

That is a God-given desire. It means you have come to see the value and blessing of fellowship with God and His people. For David, the meeting place of God was in the Tabernacle. But today, for us as believers, the Holy of Holies is open 24 hours a day, 365 days a year.

> Therefore, brothers, since we have confidence to enter the Most Holy Place by the blood of Jesus, by a new and living way opened for us through the curtain, that is, his body, and since we have a great priest over the house of God, let us draw near to God with a sincere heart in full assurance of faith. (Hebrews 10:19-22, NIV)

What an unbelievable privilege. You and I have a privilege that David and the great saints of the Old Testament could scarcely even imagine—confidence to enter the most holy place . . . drawing near to God.

You and I can worship and call on the Lord anytime, anywhere. Even a place like your car can become a sanctuary of sorts, with Bible teaching CDs, mp3 players, and worship music.

When you meditate on psalms like Psalm 27, you have to think, "No wonder God called this a man after His own heart!" His heart seemed to beat in time with the Lord's. If you want to be a man or woman after God's own heart, you would do well to learn from the priorities of David.

Not long ago, a question in a magazine advertisement caught my attention: *Is it an alarm or a calling that gets you out of bed in the morning?*

I like that question. I think it's something we need to ask ourselves often. What gets your blood pumping? What makes you tick? What is the "one thing" in your life right now? Everybody has that one thing. It might be career, money, possessions, success, or relationships.

By the way, there's nothing wrong with any of the things I just mentioned, but they should never, never become the focus and driving purpose of your life. That pursuit should be reserved for God alone. If you will order your life so that you "seek first his kingdom and his righteousness . . . all these things will be given to you as well."[51]

Is that some kind of guarantee that you will obtain all you long for on this earth? No, He doesn't promise that. But then again, He may give you more! God knows what's right, so just seek Him. You'll never be a loser for it.

David was an ordinary man and a spiritual man—both qualities that God looks for in the man or woman He uses. And there was also a third important quality. . . .

## 3. God Uses Faithful People

At this particular time in David's life, his primary responsibility was for his sheep.

Not armies. Not battles. Not kingdoms. Not alliances.

Just sheep. A flock of woolies in the wilderness.

But it was a responsibility he took very seriously. He later mentions that he went one-on-one with both lions and bears to protect those sheep—and he took them down! Out there in the open country, he would spend hours worshipping the Lord while he watched that little flock. No doubt, that is when Psalm 23 must have come to him.

*The Lord is my shepherd, I shall not want. . . .*

Just because God has called you to be a leader doesn't mean you are ready. There are always a series of tests first. It was this way before Elijah anointed Elisha . . . before Moses passed the baton to Joshua . . . before Joseph was prepared to step into a huge position of responsibility.

Young Joseph, you may remember, had been filled with visions of grandeur. He had a dream and rightly envisioned his brothers bowing before him. But some things are best kept to yourself. Perhaps God has given you a dream, a vision of what you will be.

Don't go boasting of it to everyone; just be faithful in what He has set before you. If it is really from Him it will happen, but not through your manipulation and conniving.

As we have seen, David had already been anointed. And yet instead of allowing that to change his life, he just kept on faithfully doing what he had been doing previously.

As Chuck Swindoll points out in his excellent book on David, "he didn't go down to the nearest department store and try on crowns. He didn't order a new set of business cards, telling the printer 'Change it from Shepherd to King-elect' He didn't have a badge saying, 'I'm the new Man.' Didn't shine up a chariot and race through the streets of Bethlehem yelling, 'I'm God's choice . . . You're looking at Saul's replacement!' No, he just waited for further orders."[52]

And now those orders had come. But those instructions from God didn't drop out of heaven in a golden envelope. As far as we know, there had been no dramatic vision or dream pointing the young shepherd toward the Valley of Elah and a confrontation with a Philistine champion.

It didn't happen like that. David was simply sent by his dad to carry some bread and cheese to his big brothers on the battle line. And obedient son that he was, David accepted the task without question and started on his way.

Sometimes it's funny how God works. It was faithfulness on an errand for his dad that would result in David's first big victory. David could have protested and said, "Don't you know that I'm the future king of Israel? I'm above such things! Let them find their own cheese sandwiches."

No, David was a spiritual man, a faithful and humble man, and he did what Jesse asked.

So often, that's the way God's directions come. We may be looking for some spectacular sign in the heavens or a mysterious voice in the night. More likely, however, God will call us and direct us through the simple, everyday occurrences of life. If we are walking with God and faithfully taking care of our responsibilities, He will guide our steps.

David's brothers were on the battle lines because the Israelites were facing off with their longtime enemies, the Philistines. The two armies, occupying opposing sides of the Valley of Elah, had been in a virtual standoff for days.

The main attraction during those days had been a Philistine warrior by the name of Goliath. He was a hulking freak, a giant of a man, who had been a warrior from his youth. Every day he would bellow over to the Israeli side, "What's the matter with you guys? Are you chicken? Send someone to fight me right now and this will be over. In fact, I'll make you a deal you can't refuse. If your guy can beat me, we Philistines will serve you. But if I win, Israel becomes our slaves. What do you say? Deal?"

If Goliath had been trying to get inside the Israelites' heads and psych them out, he was successful. The giant had them all— King Saul included—trembling with fear.

Enter David, the-shepherd-boy-anointed-king. And that is how David "happened" to hear the bellowing of Goliath, challenging Israelite warriors to single combat. History was about to be made, and it all started with an errand by a faithful young man.

In my life, I've found that divine opportunity usually—if not almost always—comes unexpectedly. I think of the wonderful doors God has opened for me over the years, and they always seemed to happen suddenly.

David looked at the oversized Philistine with amazement. He couldn't believe his ears. The giant was actually blaspheming the God of Israel—and no one was doing anything about it!

Goliath would have been a fear-inspiring sight. He wore a suit of armor over his nine-foot-six-inch frame—and the armor alone weighed in at 200 pounds. His massive head was covered with a bronze helmet, and he carried a huge javelin, with a head that weighed 25 pounds!

Every day this freak yelled his challenges across the valley, and every day the Israelites sank deeper into despair. This had gone on for *forty days* by the time David arrived. Israel's army was virtually paralyzed by fear.

And then the red-headed stranger showed up.

The young man who had taken on lions and bears in the wilderness couldn't believe the soldiers—including his brothers—could sit there and listen to that mockery and blasphemy day after day. David became righteously indignant. He was ready to take on Goliath right then and there.

But there was some opposition to David fighting the Philistine. So, who opposed David? The enemy? No, his own brother, Eliab. The elder son of Jesse laid into his little brother with a vengeance.

> "What are you doing around here, anyway?" he demanded. "What about the sheep you're supposed to be taking care of? I know what a cocky brat you are; you just want to see the battle!" (1 Samuel 17:28, TLB)

"What's the matter, little boy?" he mocked. "Did you get bored at home and want to play with the big boys?" Eliab was probably still smarting from the fact that God had rejected him and chosen his red-headed freckle-faced younger sibling instead.

There was Goliath, like a mouthpiece of the devil himself, taunting Israel and mocking God . . . and Eliab wanted to fight with his little brother!

This is so typical of some in the church today. Even in the face of a lost world all around us and with the end times upon us, so many in the church want to quibble over such insignificant things! When are we going to realize who the real enemy is?

David basically ignored Eliab and went to talk to the king. Saul—whom Scripture tells us was head and shoulders above everyone else in the country—should have stepped forward as Israel's champion. Standing in the presence of this failed king, David volunteered to take on Goliath singlehandedly.

Saul and his soldiers laughed at the thought of a youth like David taking on Goliath. But since they really had no other options, they finally agreed. Maybe Saul was thinking, "This kid might buy us some time. Or maybe Goliath will laugh himself to death, or trip over little David. Who knows? If nothing else, it will be pure entertainment. Go David! We're behind you one hundred percent!"

If David knew they were smirking at him, he didn't let it faze him. Instead, he prepared himself to go to war for the God he loved. And this brings us to fourth quality God looks for in the people He uses.

## 4. God Uses People Who Are Bold and Courageous.

There is a time for faithfulness, humility, and persevering through a long string of normal days. As Eugene Peterson titled one of his books, we need "a long obedience in the same direction."

But we must also remember that when God opens a door of opportunity, it can be very quick and unexpected. In our walk with Him, we will encounter situations where something must be done, said, attempted, or accomplished quickly—a divine moment that must be seized or lost forever.

When those moments come . . . *Carpe Diem.* (Seize the day!)

Maybe you are at such a place right now. You've encountered a wrong that needs to be righted. A person who needs to be spoken to. A moment that must be seized to step out in faith. There is both a time to pray and a time to get up off your knees and *move*.

David knew that Goliath had ridiculed the living God long enough. It was time to move. So he gathered five smooth stones and walked directly over to Goliath with his sling.

As the Philistine paced back and forth, his shield bearer in front of him, he noticed David. He took one look down on him and sneered—a mere youngster, apple-cheeked and peach-fuzzed.

The Philistine ridiculed David. "Am I a dog that you come after me with a stick?" And he cursed him by his gods.

"Come on," said the Philistine. "I'll make roadkill of you for the buzzards. I'll turn you into a tasty morsel for the field mice."

David answered, "You come at me with sword and spear and battle-ax. I come at you in the name of GOD-of-the-Angel-Armies, the God of Israel's troops, whom you curse and mock. This very day GOD is handing you over to me. I'm about to kill you, cut off your head, and serve up your body and the bodies of your Philistine buddies to the crows and coyotes. The whole earth will know that there's an extraordinary God in Israel. And everyone gathered here will learn that GOD doesn't save by means of sword or spear. The battle belongs to GOD—he's handing you to us on a platter!"

That roused the Philistine, and he started toward David. David took off from the front line, running toward the Philistine. David reached into his pocket for a stone, slung it, and hit the Philistine hard in the forehead, embedding the stone deeply. The Philistine crashed, facedown in the dirt.

That's how David beat the Philistine—with a sling and a stone. He hit him and killed him. No sword for David!

Then David ran up to the Philistine and stood over him, pulled the giant's sword from its sheath, and finished the job by cutting off his head. When the Philistines saw that their great champion was dead, they scattered, running for their lives. (1 Samuel 17:41-51, THE MESSAGE)

God is still looking for men and women—ordinary people—willing to do extraordinary things. But as with David, you must be a truly spiritual person and have a heart that is fixed on God. You must be willing to be faithful in the little things, but also bold and courageous.

And when the moment comes . . . *seize it!*

## chapter seven
# David's Story, Part 2: The Power of Forgiveness

"Who am I that you pay attention to a stray dog like me?"
—2 Samuel 9:8, THE MESSAGE

We've all experienced it. When the holidays come, we suddenly find ourselves thrown into close quarters with relatives we may not have seen for months, even years. We're rubbing shoulders with cousins we didn't know we had, in-laws we wanted to forget, aunts who drive us nuts, and uncles who always tell the same dumb stories.

You may have some issues of genuine pain in your family. You've been wounded at some point—deeply hurt—by the people who should have loved you most, and the holidays only remind you of that. Children have been disappointed with parents, and parents with children. Husbands have been let down by wives, and wives by husbands. Petty squabbles turn into long-standing rivalries and feuds. The bitterness at times can run very deep.

Maybe it was the way someone handled family money.

Maybe it was some angry words—spoken long ago, and long remembered.

Maybe someone deliberately slandered you, telling lies and hurting your reputation.

So how should you handle this?

In a word, *forgive.*

You say, "But they don't deserve forgiveness!" That may be true. But since when did what we "deserve" enter the equation? Would you really like to be judged by God on the basis of what you deserve?

C. S. Lewis wrote that "everyone says forgiveness is a lovely idea, until they have something to forgive." But by harboring resentment and refusing to forgive, we grieve the Holy Spirit.

And do not bring sorrow to God's Holy Spirit by the way you live. Remember, he has identified you as his own, guaranteeing that you will be saved on the day of redemption.

Get rid of all bitterness, rage, anger, harsh words, and slander, as well as all types of evil behavior. Instead, be kind to each other, tenderhearted, forgiving one another, just as God through Christ has forgiven you.
(Ephesians 4:30-32, NLT)

God's command to forgive should be enough, but let me give you an additional reason . . . you may live longer! A new field of research has been developed on the subject of forgiveness. Recent studies suggest that those who do not forgive are more likely to experience high blood pressure, bouts of depression, and problems with anger, stress, and anxiety.

Charlotte van Oyen Witvliet of Hope College in Holland, Michigan has found that there are robust physiological differences between non-forgiving and forgiving states in those she has studied. "If you are willing to exert the effort it takes to be forgiving," says Witvliet, "there are benefits both emotionally and physically."

As many of these studies are beginning to illustrate, forgiveness is not about absolving the perpetrator; it is about healing the victim. "Forgiveness isn't giving in to another person, it's getting free of that person" said Frederic Luskin, director of the Stanford Forgiveness Project.

God knew what He was talking about when He told us to forgive!

Many people think that the Old Testament is all about vengeance and harsh justice, while the New Testament owns the concept of forgiveness. And yet the Old Testament book of 1 Samuel relates one of the most moving stories of forgiveness in the Bible. It's a story of how David dealt with his enemies when "payback time" finally came.

# A Surprise Choice

Saul, as we have already seen in an earlier chapter, was the ruler God gave to Israel after they had begged and whined for a king so they "could be like all the other nations." So the Lord gave them just what *they* wanted (not always such a good thing), a tall, handsome, charismatic man after their own heart.

All too soon, however, Israel's first king became paranoid and vengeful, misusing his office and dishonoring the Lord who had elevated him to such prominence. Before his reign was really up and rolling, he'd already forfeited the kingship.

David, a youthful, clear-eyed shepherd who loved the Lord with all his heart, was God's surprise choice for Saul's successor. After slaying Goliath in the Valley of Elah, the youngest son of Jesse became an instant folk hero with the people. If Israel had radio in those days, a new song about David would have topped the charts. Everyone was singing it . . . and particularly the women!

So the women sang as they danced, and said:

"Saul has slain his thousands,
And David his ten thousands."
(1 Samuel 18:7)

David struck up a very strong friendship with Saul's son Jonathan. Prince Jonathan, a good and valorous young man, knew very well that God's hand was on David. Under normal circumstances, Jonathan could have expected to receive the kingship from his father. But these weren't normal circumstances, and the young prince could see the handwriting on the wall. Rather than being filled with resentment and jealousy, however, Jonathan simply asked his friend to remember his decedents after his death.

Meanwhile, Saul was on a collision course with his destiny. Overcome with hatred and jealousy, he tried to kill David over and over.

In other words, once David was selected by God, his troubles began! It's often the same for you and me. There's no doubt that making a conscious decision to follow Jesus Christ transforms any life for the better, filling the emptiness in your life and washing away sin and guilt. You're given an entirely new dimension of life to live. You now have a God who will guide and counsel you and direct you through all the ups and downs of life, and best of all, you have the hope of heaven!

But while one complete set of problems ceases to exist, an entirely new set of problems begins! Conversion makes our heart into a battlefield. But the good news is that God will be with us, never giving us more than we can handle.

> Can anything ever separate us from Christ's love? Does it mean he no longer loves us if we have trouble or calamity, or are persecuted, or hungry, or destitute, or in danger, or threatened with death? (As the Scriptures say, "For your sake we are killed every day; we are being slaughtered like sheep.") No, despite all these things, overwhelming victory is ours through Christ, who loved us.
>
> And I am convinced that nothing can ever separate us from God's love. Neither death nor life, neither angels nor demons, neither our fears for today nor our worries about tomorrow—not even the powers of hell can separate us from God's love. No power in the sky above or in the earth below—indeed, nothing in all creation will ever be able to separate us from the love of God that is revealed in Christ Jesus our Lord. (Romans 8:35-39, NLT)

For absolutely no reason beyond Saul's insane jealousy, David was forced into exile—and this after the king had twice tried to pin him to the wall with a spear.

As Saul and his army chased David from one end of Israel to the other, David had a couple of golden opportunities to kill this crazy man. Once, at a place called Engedi, Saul entered a dark cave to "answer the call of nature."

The king laid aside his robe and there he was, as vulnerable as can be, within easy reach of David's sword (and what a humiliating way to go).

Instead of running Saul through, however, David used his sword to cut off part of his royal robe. After Saul left the cave, David called to him, "Do you feel a draft, King Saul? I could have killed you but I didn't! The Lord judge between you and I and the Lord avenge me of you!"[53]

Saul, suddenly realizing how close he had been to his doom, called back to David.

> "Is this your voice , my son David?" And Saul lifted up his voice and wept. Then he said to David: "You are more righteous than I; for you have rewarded me with good, whereas I have rewarded you with evil. . . . Now I know indeed that you shall surely be king, and that the kingdom of Israel shall be established in your hand." (1 Samuel 24:16-17, 20)

But in spite of such assurances, Saul tried again and again to eliminate his perceived rival. The once promising king utterly threw away his life, ending up so desperate and spiritually bankrupt that he sought counsel from a witch.

Finally, the wicked Saul reaped what he had sown. He died on the battlefield alongside his son Jonathan. The words on his tombstone could have very well read, "I have played the fool!" Actually, Saul committed suicide on the battlefield, falling on his own sword.

A short time later, some fool approached David, claiming to have killed the king. Outraged, David had this man executed. The House of Saul and the House of David, however, continued in war for a number of years. Saul had another son named Ishbosheth, and Abner, Saul's general, made him king.

Not long after this, Abner and Isbosheth had an argument, and the general threatened to defect. Sure enough, he went to David and offered to unite the kingdom under him. After all the misery Abner had caused David, he could have struck the military man dead.

But instead David accepted the offer and gave Abner and his men a great feast.

David was simply tired of the fighting, and he longed for peace. When Joab, David's general, returned, he was outraged. He hunted Abner down and murdered him. Stunned by this vicious act of violence, David went into deep mourning.

The plot continued to thicken! Later, a couple of men loyal to David assassinated Ishbosheth, Saul's son. Coming to David with the news and expecting to be rewarded, the king dealt as harshly with them as he had with the man who had claimed he killed Saul.

Here's where all of this is leading.

*David did not deal with his enemies the way they dealt with him.* He believed in justice and mercy. He dealt with those who wanted to exploit the situation with justice, but he dealt with those who were innocently caught in the crossfire with forgiveness.

Without the benefit of psychologists or intensive academic and university studies, David understood the power of forgiveness.

Maybe you, too, have been persecuted wrongfully by someone, or have an enemy who has tried to do you harm. Perhaps you still feel the bruises from someone who turned against you or spread lies about you.

How would you feel about these adversaries if their personal attacks against you—totally undeserved—affected your life for *years?* Now . . . imagine yourself emerging on the other side of the dark tunnel after all this hurt and harassment. Would your first thought be of how you could show kindness to that person or to any of their family?

Well, that's exactly what David did.

## Remembering His Promise

Some time after David had been established on his throne over all Israel, firmly in power, he remembered something. It was a promise he had made to both King Saul and Prince Jonathan. On different occasions, he had sworn an oath to both men to show kindness and mercy to their descendants. But were any of them still alive?

What follows in Scripture truly is one the greatest stories ever told!

(David) summoned a man named Ziba, who had been one of Saul's servants. "Are you Ziba?" the king asked.

"Yes sir, I am," Ziba replied.

The king then asked him, "Is anyone still alive from Saul's family? If so, I want to show God's kindness to them."

Ziba replied, "Yes, one of Jonathan's sons is still alive. He is crippled in both feet."

"Where is he?" the king asked.

"In Lo-debar," Ziba told him, "at the home of Makir son of Ammiel."

So David sent for him and brought him from Makir's home. His name was Mephibosheth; he was Jonathan's son and Saul's grandson. When he came to David, he bowed low to the ground in deep respect. David said, "Greetings, Mephi-bosheth."

Mephibosheth replied, "I am your servant."

"Don't be afraid!" David said. "I intend to show kindness to you because of my promise to your father, Jonathan. I will give you all the property that once belonged to your grandfather Saul, and you will eat here with me at the king's table!"

Mephibosheth bowed respectfully and exclaimed, "Who is your servant, that you should show such kindness to a dead dog like me?"

. . . And from that time on, Mephibosheth ate regularly at David's table, like one of the king's own sons. . . . And Mephibosheth, who was crippled in both feet, lived in Jerusalem and ate regularly at the king's table. (2 Samuel 9:2-8, 11, 13)

This story may not have the dramatic elements of Samson's story—or the sagas of Gideon or Joshua, either. It's more subtle, but beautiful and tender. Here is David, who after years of struggle with the house of Saul is finally crowned king of Israel—perhaps fifteen years after he was anointed in Bethlehem.

Under normal circumstances, kings in that era would seek to eliminate any potential rivals to the throne. What would you have done in similar circumstances? Is your motto, "I don't get mad, I get even"? Even though he was disabled, Mephibosheth, grandson of Saul and the son of Prince Jonathan, would have been next in line for the throne if Saul's family was still ruling. As a matter of fact, this young man was still a potential threat to David's crown as long as he was alive. Yet David reached out to a potential rival, even an enemy, and loved him.

No wonder David was called "a man after God's own heart"!

## A Shadowed Life

Mephibosheth was only five years old when his father and grandfather were killed. Imagine, if you will, the life he had known up until then. The privilege and potential of his present could not have prepared him for the hard life he would have to face in his future.

Raised as a young prince in the royal residence by a brave and godly father, Mephibosheth had no inkling of the dark clouds gathering all around his small world. And then, in just one moment of carelessness and through no fault of his own, his life was changed forever.

When the news hit the palace of his father and grandfather's deaths, the nurse in charge hurried to take Mephibosheth—heir to throne—into hiding. In her haste, however, she would add even more tragedy to the story. Somehow she dropped the young child, crippling his legs for the rest of his life.

His name, literally translated, means "a shameful thing." There was nothing little Mephiposheth had done to earn this name, but he was looked down upon. Now crippled, with no hope of gaining the throne, he was regarded as a worthless person.

Maybe sometime in your growing-up years you were dropped too. As a child you were mistreated, neglected, abused, and forgotten, like so many kids today who have basically been left to themselves. Maybe people haven't given you much hope. You've been written off by parents, coaches, and teachers.

I have some good news for you today. God specializes in taking people who have been dropped in life and picking them back up again!

I read about how Walt Disney, as a young man, was fired from his job at a newspaper. When Disney asked why, his supervisor bluntly replied, "Walt, you're not creative enough. You never have any new ideas. We're sorry, but we're going to have to let you go."

Disney got dropped in life. But instead of giving up and withdrawing into himself, he moved to California, borrowed $500, and started a graphics arts company in a garage. Shortly after, he came up with a little character he named Mortimer Mouse . . . later to become Mickey. And the rest is history.

Mephibosheth was dropped in life. And all through his years he may have lived as a fugitive in fear of King David. No doubt he had been told the circumstances of his crippling fall. Maybe he blamed all his woes on the upstart king. If it weren't for David, he would be whole and complete and seated on his grandfather's throne. Perhaps he lay awake some nights, wondering if the king knew about his existence. Would he wake up to the sound of soldiers some night, banging on the door where he lived? That would be the end for him and his family. He would be called to the palace to pay with his life for the actions of his grandfather.

Mephibosheth would have been taught to hate David. How could he have ever imagined that the king was seeking the welfare of someone from Saul's family?

David asked Saul's former servant, "Is there still anyone who is left of the house of Saul, that I may show him kindness for Jonathan's sake?" (2 Samuel 9:1).

The word "kindness" in this verse could better be translated *grace*. David was saying, "Is there someone of Saul's household I could show grace to?" Grace is positive and unconditional acceptance in spite of the other person. It is a demonstration of love that is undeserved, unearned, and un-repayable.

*"Is there any relative of Jonathan I can show unconditional love to?"*

A man named Ziba mentions Mephibosheth. But notice what he says. "There is still a son of Jonathan; he is crippled in both feet" (2 Samuel 9:3, NIV). I don't think it's reading too much into the text if I paraphrase Ziba's words to say: "Yes, O King, there is someone. But you many want to reconsider your offer. He is crippled. Disabled. Handicapped. He can't reciprocate your kindness."

It's never easy to be disabled. But in this era of history, it was just plain awful. There were no wheelchairs, no handicapped access to buildings, no reserved parking places. Mephibosheth would have had to be carried everywhere. To the table. To the restroom. To his bedroom. To wherever he wanted to go! In essence, Ziba is saying, "Do you really want to take on this responsibility? This isn't your problem, King!"

Do you think that mattered to David? Not at all! Love is not based on the worthiness of the object. So Ziba complies with David's request and tells him where Mephibosheth lives; a place called Lo-debar, located in a relatively obscure spot on the east side of the Jordan River.

The former of prince of Israel was living in some barren corner in the middle of nowhere. This wasn't a fit place for a child of a king to be living. Lo-debar means literally, "the place of no pasture." What a pathetic picture we have of Jonathan's son. Isolated from worship at the Tabernacle, cut off from fellowship, unable to walk or live an independent life, and living out his life in a barren place. It wasn't an easy life—nor a happy one.

It's also a picture of each of us before we gave our lives to Jesus Christ. Hanging out in Lo-debar . . . living like low-lifes . . . feeling unloved, unwanted, undeserving, and unneeded.

But just as David reached out in grace and kindness to Mephibosheth, so God reaches out to us. The Bible says that "while we were still sinners, Christ died for us."[54]

So King David sent for the forgotten Prince Mephibosheth and brought him from Makir's home to Jerusalem. David was persistent, not giving up on this young man. He didn't just send for him, but *brought* him.

Here is a reminder of how persistent we should be when reaching out with the gospel. Jesus told us to "Go out to the roads and country lanes and make them come in, so that my house will be full."[55]

Remember the story of the four men who brought their paralyzed friend to Jesus, practically ripping the roof off the house where He was speaking because they couldn't get in the door? Remember how Andrew brought his brother Peter to Jesus? God shows the same loving persistence toward you and me.

In this story of the crippled prince, David, like Jesus, shows forgiveness and love instead of judgment. Though Mephibosheth had personally done nothing wrong (that we know of), his grandfather had tried to murder David—for years and years!

But David had made a promise he intended to keep.

So how did Mephibosheth react when he heard David wanted to see him? He was afraid! Under normal circumstances, he would have been justified to have that fear. After all, Mephibosheth's point of reference was his wicked grandfather. It was customary for eastern kings to not only kill all rivals to their throne, but to exterminate their heirs as well.

Bottom line, Mephibosheth simply didn't know David. If the young prince had known this man of God, he wouldn't have been afraid. This was a new king with a new heart. He was a man who began as a shepherd boy, became a giant-killer, then endured long, lean years of struggle and hardship as a fugitive. But he was man who grew into his calling and title, "a man after God's heart."

In the same way, there are many people who are afraid of God today. We think He's out to get us or make our lives miserable.

We imagine that His main purpose toward us is imposing a bunch of restrictive rules and regulations that will hem us in and turn our lives from living color to black-and-white. What a false and warped perception of God! A. W. Tozer writes, "Nothing twists and deforms the soul more than a low or unworthy conception of God."

David brought Mephibosheth into his royal family, "and Mephibosheth lived in Jerusalem, because he always ate at the king's table" (2 Samuel 9:13, NIV).

In just thirteen verses in 2 Samuel 9, the Bible mentions the word "eat" or "ate" four times. Yes, eating is a necessary biological function to sustain life. But in Scripture, it's often much more than that; it is a time of fellowship, sharing, and rejoicing.

Jesus' first miracle was performed at a wedding feast. The last thing Jesus did after His resurrection and just before His ascension was to cook fish over coals and eat a meal with His disciples. None of us wants to go to dinner with a person we really don't know or don't like. (It can give you indigestion). That's why blind dates are such a drag! Most of us like to dine with family and friends, people we're comfortable with and enjoy.

Listen to the Lord's invitation in the book of Revelation:

Look! I stand at the door and knock. If you hear my voice and open the door, I will come in, and we will share a meal together as friends. (Revelation 3:20, NLT)

When the day finally came for Mephibosheth to meet David, he was gripped with apprehension. For the first time in his life, he would see the man whom his grandfather hunted mercilessly for years and regarded as Public Enemy Number One.

After David's kind words and incredibly generous offer, Mephibosheth bowed down, realizing he had been dead wrong in allowing the prejudice of others to influence his own attitude.

Let's draw a few lessons from this story as we wrap it up.

# What We Learn from the Story

## Lesson 1:
## Don't let others form your view of God.

Find out for yourself who God is. Mephibosheth allowed the prejudice and bias of others to keep him from a generous king and provider. So many are kept from a relationship with God by what others say. I recently spoke to a young woman struggling with drugs. She placed the blame for her problems on her parents. In the course of our conversation, I warned her not to form her view of God based solely on the attitudes and actions of her mother and father.

We parents will inevitably disappoint, make mistakes, and get it wrong many times. But not God. He always gets it right. And when He looks on you as His child, He smiles with delight!

God loves you, and His plan for you is better than any you could ever come up with for yourself. Don't run from Him, but to Him. Sit at His table and enjoy His company. Nobody has a greater interest in your life than He does, and He has all the time in the world for you. He says to you, "I know the plans I have for you. . . . They are plans for good and not for disaster, to give you a future and a hope" (Jeremiah 29:11, NLT).

## Lesson 2: Forgive your enemies.

Forgive them whether they deserve it or not.

David could have engaged in payback, big time, hunting down everyone who had ever been associated with Saul and his reign. But he did the very opposite, endearing him to all of Israel.

Abraham Lincoln was once criticized by an associate for his attitude toward political enemies. The associate asked, "Why do you always make friends of them? You should destroy them!" Lincoln replied, "Am I not destroying my enemies when I make them my friends?"

Paul writes:

Repay no one evil for evil. Have regard for good things in the sight of all men. If it is possible, as much as depends on you, live peaceably with all men. Beloved, do not avenge yourselves, but rather give place to wrath; for it is written, "Vengeance is Mine, I will repay," says the Lord. Therefore, "If your enemy is hungry, feed him; if he is thirsty, give him a drink; for in so doing you will heap coals of fire on his head" (Romans 12:17-20).

When the right time came, God took care of the enemies of David. He didn't have to lift a finger.

## Lesson 3: Leave the past in the past.

David could have spent the rest of his life stewing over what had happened or what others had done to him. He lost at least fifteen prime years of his life hiding in caves and running from Saul—and he was totally innocent!

Think of what could have happened as a result of all those injustices. David could have shriveled up inside, becoming a bitter, negative man. But he didn't, as the story in this chapter reveals. He came through those dark days with a kind and tender heart still intact. He could have become angry at God, turning away from the Lord because He didn't rescue him and elevate him sooner. But we all know that didn't happen either. All you have to do is open up the Psalms, and you see that David's love and heart for the Lord just grew and grew.

In fact, it was those lonely years of hiding in the wilderness where David would experience God as his Refuge, Rock, Deliverer, and Strong Tower.

As a man after God's heart, David knew God was in control of his life, no matter how difficult the circumstances. He wrote:

But as for me, I trust in You, O LORD;
I say, "You are my God."
My times are in Your hand;

Deliver me from the hand of my enemies,
And from those who persecute me.
(Psalm 31:14-15)

Even though he didn't enjoy suffering any more than you and
I enjoy it, David knew the Lord was allowing what he was experiencing to prepare him for the future, both good and bad.

The funny thing about life is that what we initially think is
"good" may turn out in time to be "bad." And that which seems
so bad right now may turn out to be very, very good.

The Bible says of God: "He has made everything beautiful in its
time. Also, he has put eternity into man's heart, yet so that he cannot find out what God has done from the beginning to the end."[56]

Bottom line, even though he had been victimized, David
refused to be a victim. Through everything that happened to him
in his life, he kept his focus on the Lord, giving Him his trust and
devotion.

The story of David and Mephibosheth is a picture of what
God has done for us.

First, out of sheer love for Jonathan, David lavished his grace
on his friend's handicapped son. It reminds me of how God, out
of love for His Son, Jesus Christ, paid the price for our sin at
Calvary. He's still seeking those who are spiritually handicapped,
people locked in destructive lifestyles of sin. God has sought us
out, calling us to His table.

Second, Mephibosheth had nothing, deserved nothing, and
could repay nothing. In fact, He was hiding from the king. The
same is true of us. We were willful, intentional sinners, yet Jesus
sought us out and called our name.

Third, Mephibosheth was adopted as a son and invited to eat
at the king's table for the rest of his life. We have been adopted
into God's family. We have not received the spirit of bondage
again to fear, but one of adoption.[57]

God has made us a part of His eternal family. We are invited
to be near Him, to be with Him, to find purpose and joy in His
service, and to share in the bounty of His table.

That, my friend, is grace.

## chapter eight

# David's Story, Part 3:
# The God of Second Chances

"Then Nathan said to David, 'You are the man!' "
—2 Samuel 12:7

retailers make it *so* easy for you to part with your money. You can buy furniture and not pay a dime for a year.

You can buy a car for no money down and with easy monthly payments . . . for the next seventeen years.

And of course you can charge everything under the sun— from a cheeseburger, to your groceries, to your new high-powered laptop, to your dental work, to your pet vaccinations.

It's so easy. It's so convenient. In years past, people actually had to set money aside and save up for things they wanted. Can you imagine? They didn't buy something until they had enough money, then they went in and laid the cash on the counter. What an archaic notion!

But in all of that retail ease and convenience to which we've become accustomed, there is something we tend to forget.

The bills *will* come due.

We *will* still pay.

In our third look at King David in this book, we come to the story of a man who made a big grab for gratification . . . and then paid a very, very steep price. King that he was, David found out that no one is above the law—God's law, that is. He may have thought he could sin and never pay, but he was wrong. And when the bills came due, he owed more than he ever dreamed.

Plucked from obscurity, David became the greatest king in the history of Israel. Who can forget his dramatic rise from shepherd boy to giant-killer?

When the years of running and hiding from jealous King Saul were finally over, David stepped into his destiny, ruling first over his own tribe of Judah, and then over the whole nation of Israel.

Recognizing God's hand on their leader, the people loved him. And David, at least in the beginning, was humble enough to recognize that God was the source of his success. He truly loved the Lord and wanted to stay close to Him and serve Him. In all of this, David lived up to the Lord's description of him as a man after God's own heart!

Everything was going so beautifully.

But then he got sloppy.

It started with a lustful look and ended up as a nationwide scandal. Though David's initial sin with Bathsheba lasted only minutes, the repercussions of it lasted for the rest of His life. No sin, except perhaps the original sin of Adam and Eve, has received as much press as David's adultery with Bathsheba. But we must not forget as we read this story, sordid as it is, that David was still called a man after God's own heart.

That is not in any way to justify David's actions, for it was a terrible wrong and broke the heart of God. But it is a reminder to us that if someone as beloved of God as David could fall, so could anyone . . . including you or me.

## Satan Sets the Trap

In the spring of the year, when kings normally go out to war, David sent Joab and the Israelite army to fight the Ammonites. They destroyed the Ammonite army and laid siege to the city of Rabbah. However, David stayed behind in Jerusalem.

Late one afternoon, after his midday rest, David got out of bed and was walking on the roof of the palace. As he looked out over the city, he noticed a woman of unusual beauty taking a bath. He sent someone to find out who she was, and he was told, "She is Bathsheba, the daughter of Eliam and the wife of Uriah the Hittite."

Then David sent messengers to get her; and when she came to the palace, he slept with her. She had just completed the purification rites after having her menstrual period. Then she returned home. Later, when Bathsheba discovered that she was pregnant, she sent David a message, saying, "I'm pregnant." (2 Samuel 11:1-5, NLT)

David was about fifty years old when this incident took place. He had ruled Israel for twenty years, moving from victory to victory, with success and God's favor at every turn. He had distinguished himself as a wise and compassionate ruler, a man of God, a fierce general, a skilled musician, and a gifted poet, writing beautiful psalms of praise to God.

No doubt about it, King David was on a roll, and paradoxically . . . that's a time when we really need to be on our guard. When we're walking through a time of crisis, we naturally look to the Lord for help and guidance. But when life sails along smoothly on a calm sea, with no clouds on the horizon, we tend to become careless. We lower our guard . . . and the devil pounces.

Remember when Jesus faced that period of intense temptation when he went one-on-one with the devil in the wilderness? When did that happen? Right after His baptism, where the heavens opened, the Spirit descended upon Him like a dove, and a voice from the deep blue said, "This is my beloved Son. . . ."

After the dove came the devil.

After the blessing comes the trial.

The two often go hand in hand. So when you walk out of church feeling blessed, encouraged, and spiritually well fed, don't be surprised if you find temptation and testing waiting in the wings.

Odd as it may seem, Satan usually hits us when we're enjoying God's rich blessings. He waits for that moment when we are the most vulnerable—though we may imagine it to be a time in our lives when we're at our strongest and best!

David had already set the scene for his defeat by actions he had done in direct disobedience to God. This reminds us that the sins we commit today may not have their full impact on us until much later. David didn't fall suddenly; as with everyone, it was a process.

Second Samuel 5 tells us that in defiance to God's laws, David took concubines after he became king. God specifically said in Deuteronomy 17 that the future king was never to do this. The reason: "Neither shall he multiply wives for himself, lest his heart turn away. . . ."[58]

That was exactly what was happening to David—his heart was slowly but surely turning away from God.

David was allowing lust to consume his life. He might have thought it was justified because he had such a strong sexual drive. He may have thought, "Having all these wives and concubines will satisfy me." But the truth is, it only stoked the fire.

There is a difference between a healthy, God-given sex drive and being gripped with lust. God has given sexual desires to every man and woman, to be fulfilled in a monogamous marriage commitment. Without such built-in sexual attraction, the human race would have died out!

But when a man is filled with lust, as David seemed to be, he cannot satisfy it with more lust. That's like throwing gasoline on a bonfire. You show me a person who is having a serious lust problem, and I'll show you someone who *feeds* it. It may be pornography, music with explicit lyrics, friends who are preoccupied with immorality, or all of the above.

Sometimes I counsel people who seem completely mystified by all the lustful thoughts they keep having. For some reason, they don't make the connection between what they allow themselves to see or hear and what keeps dominating their thoughts. The truth is, when you don't feed lust, you starve it! David had been feeding his lust with all these women he had at his beck and call. Godly people in the kingdom were no doubt becoming aware of this. Yet they may have whispered to one another, "Oh well, it could be worse. Besides, look at all the good he's done."

If David had only realized it, he had been fattening himself up for the kill. And of course it happened when he least expected it . . . on a quiet, warm spring afternoon as he strolled on his rooftop.

## The Trap Is Sprung

Late one afternoon, after his midday rest, David got out of bed and was walking on the roof of the palace. As he looked out over the city, he noticed a woman of unusual beauty taking a bath. (2 Samuel 11:2, NLT)

Instead of leading his troops in war, David sent a proxy so he could kick back and take life easy. He was in bed when he should have been in battle. There's nothing wrong with a little R & R, as long as we remember that there *is* no rest from spiritual battle. Hell never takes a vacation.

Our greatest battles don't usually come when we're working hard; they come when we have some leisure time on our hands, when we're bored.

Alan Redpath once observed, "Times of leisure are to be more dreaded than those of the most strenuous toil."

Late one afternoon David got up from a nap, stretched, and decided to walk up to the palace rooftop for a little fresh air. It sounds like he had been burning the midnight oil, allowing himself to sleep in.

While Israel's troops were in the field, David was lounging around in his royal pajamas, catching some sun at the palace. And while he was out on his rooftop, just idly looking down at the city, David saw a beautiful woman bathing herself.

To be honest, this would have been a temptation for any healthy man, but for a man who had already fed the fire of lust, it was deadly. There's no record that David even struggled over what to do. He swiftly took action to take this woman for himself.

All rational thinking went out the door; he was like an animal driven by his lust for what he wanted. Repercussions, reputation, even fear of God, went by the wayside. He wanted this woman!

So he dispatched a servant to find out who she was.

> The man said, "Isn't this Bathsheba, the daughter of Eliam and the wife of Uriah the Hittite?"[59]

In other words, this courageous servant said, "King David, this is a married woman!" It seems that this servant could see what David was thinking (perhaps even more than David). When deluded by sin, we are often the last to realize what we are doing and where we are heading. Sin makes us stupid! We manage to rationalize every step, convincing ourselves it's really okay.

Then some Christian comes along and says, "What in the world are you doing? Why are you compromising your life like this?" Set back on our heels by such remarks, we're offended. *The nerve of that person! How judgmental can you get?*

As we read in an earlier chapter, Samson was the last to know that God's hand was no longer upon him. When Delilah had finally worn him down and he revealed the secret of his strength, she cried, "The Philistines are upon you, Samson." He rose up to cast off his enemies like rag dolls, as he had done before, but he didn't realize that the Spirit of the Lord had departed from him.

If David had been spiritually alert at all, he would have seen this servant's comment as a red flag. A warning. *"King David, this is a married woman. Married to one of your warriors who is fighting for his country at this moment."*

Probably at some later point in his life, David would write:

> Let a righteous man strike me—it is a kindness;
> let him rebuke me—it is oil on my head.
> My head will not refuse it.[60]

There would come a time when David would realize the value of strict accountability—a friend who would be willing to hit him with the truth, even if it felt like a blow to the head. (You have to wonder how it would have been for David if Prince Jonathan had lived.) But at this point in his life, he blew right on past all of God's red flags, and David had Bathsheba brought to the palace.

# Don't Become a Stumbling Block

Scripture says of Bathsheba, "The woman was very beautiful in appearance," and the Bible does not exaggerate. This means she was a knockout, drop-dead stunning! It's important to note that she shared in this sin, too. We have no record of Bathsheba protesting or fighting the king's advances, nor do we read of David forcing himself on her. It appears that she was a willing accomplice.

A modest Hebrew woman would not bathe in a place where she could be seen. Could it be Bathsheba knew she was in eyeshot of the king and hoped he might look her way? It's not enough to simply avoid sin in our lives; we must also take care that we are not a stumbling block to others.

> Yes, each of us will give a personal account to God. So let's stop condemning each other. Decide instead to live in such a way that you will not cause another believer to stumble and fall. (Romans 14:12-13, NLT)

Another translation puts it like this: "Here's what you need to be concerned about: that you don't get in the way of someone else, making life more difficult than it already is."[61]

Granted, if David had attended to his duties and gone to war, he would not have seen Bathsheba that fateful afternoon. But at the same time, if she had given more thought to her actions, she would not have put temptation in his path. If lustful looking is bad, then those who dress and expose themselves with the desire to be looked at and lusted after are not less, but perhaps more, guilty!

Girls and women . . . think about what you are wearing (or not wearing) before you leave your house. How would you feel if it was Jesus who was taking you out somewhere? That doesn't mean you can't be in style. But don't dress in such a way as to encourage a guy to lust after you.

You might protest, "But Greg, some guys would lust after a *tree!*" True. But that doesn't excuse you from practicing some modesty.

I think Paul nailed it for all of us when he wrote:

Be very careful, then, how you live—not as unwise but as wise . . . because the days are evil. Therefore do not be foolish, but understand what the Lord's will is. (Ephesians 5:15-17, NIV)

Neither David nor Bathsheba walked carefully in this incident, and both, I believe, were at fault. As it is so often said, *It takes two to tango.*

Even so, David was clearly the aggressor here. He stopped, looked, lusted, and acted on his sin. And because he was king and had the power, he used it.

## A Tangled Web

You have to jump through a lot of hoops to end up in adultery. You don't just fall into someone's bed. You have to go beyond mere lust, and begin to plot and scheme and lie. The awful betrayal in this sin is more than the act itself, it's in all the prep work and attempts to hide it.

David probably enjoyed himself on this night of sinful pleasure. It's just like that expensive toy you buy for yourself and play with for a week or two. Then the bill comes due, and you have already moved on to other conquests. And then to add insult to injury, the bill comes due with interest.

That's how sin works. There is that initial high, that rush of excitement. After all, the Bible says there is pleasure in sin for a time. But Scripture also reminds us that your sin will find you out!

Not long after his one night stand with Bathsheba, she sends him a note that says, "David, I'm pregnant!"

Here now is the second obstacle or red-flag warning David should have paid attention to. When it dawned on him that he had actually impregnated another man's wife, he should have repented before God and come clean. If he had confessed before God and men *right then*, there certainly would have been some pain and anger and messy complications. But the end of the story might have turned out very differently.

I can imagine Uriah taking his wife, moving to Beersheba, and raising the child as his own.

But instead, David did what most people try to do when they're caught in sin. *They try to cover it up.* But there is something about sin that just doesn't want to stay covered. Remember Moses murdering the Egyptian and burying him in the sand? All it took was a good stiff wind to reveal what he had done.

## Deadly Cover–up

Of all the people caught in adultery over the years, I cannot think of one who willingly admitted it. They only admit it when confronted with the evidence—and even then they may try to deny it.

So the plot began to thicken right away. David asked his top general, Joab, to call in Bathsheba's courageous husband, Uriah, who had been fighting the king's battle at Rabbah. So the unsuspecting soldier was sent home and ordered to report to the king.

How excited he must have been! *Why would the King of Israel, a man after God's own heart, summon someone like me? What a privilege and honor!*

Poor Uriah. He would have never dreamed of David's true motives. After a little small talk, David asked Uriah how the battle was going. Then he told him to go home to his wife (nod, nod, wink, wink). But Uriah was such a man of integrity he could not justify this luxury when his fellow soldiers were still fighting for the king. So he wrapped himself up in his cloak and slept outside the palace.

Now what?

David found out what had happened, and invited Uriah to the palace again, this time getting him drunk. Still, Uriah slept outside the palace. This was the third red-flag warning on David's collision course with destruction. He should have seen it and repented. He had Uriah right there! What if he had confessed and rid his soul of that awful weight? It would have been initially very difficult and embarrassing, but what grief it would have saved!

Have you ever sensed God putting up roadblocks in your life to keep you from going a certain direction or pursuing a certain course? Perhaps you've been contemplating a certain sin—adultery, stealing, or cheating on your taxes. You've been rationalizing it in your mind, but God has not made it easy. That's because He loves you! That conviction, that guilt you feel in your heart, is actually a gift of mercy from God.

We have smoke detectors in our homes that sound the alarm when they sense smoke and chirp annoyingly when they need a battery. Sometimes—just to stop the racket—someone may foolishly pull out the batteries and disable the devices. And there are times when we want to do the same for our conscience.

David, instead of heeding God's red flags, dreamed up the most wicked scheme of all. At this point, David's sin had gone beyond lust, adultery, and deception.

Now he was planning a murder.

David sent Uriah back to battle with a letter he was to deliver to General Joab. No doubt Uriah felt proud and happy to be carrying a message from his king. How could he know that it was his death warrant? The orders were for the Israeli army to attack, and then for everyone to fall back, leaving poor Uriah standing alone.

I wonder what Joab thought when he read this letter. Strange how David could write such beautiful psalms and dance before the Ark of God with all his might—*and write a letter like this.* Man after God's own heart, my foot!

Brave Uriah died in battle that day, and after a brief period of mourning, Bathsheba married King David and came to live in the palace. It certainly looked as though everything was working out, and that David and Bathsheba had successfully covered up a potential scandal.

But David forgot to take God into account. And the Bible says that "the thing that David had done displeased the Lord" (2 Samuel 11:27).

# David's Broken Heart

In spite of his extreme wickedness in this incident, David was still a believer—although a very disobedient one. Deep down, David had known this was a sin before God. In later years, he would write two psalms—Psalms 32 and 51—about the agony of guilt and regret he endured following his sin.

> Oh, what joy for those whose disobedience is forgiven,
> whose sin is put out of sight!
> Yes, what joy for those whose record
> the LORD has cleared of guilt,
> whose lives are lived in complete honesty!
>
> When I refused to confess my sin,
> My body wasted away,
> and I groaned all day long.
> Day and night your hand of discipline was heavy on me.
> My strength evaporated like water in the summer heat.
>
> Finally, I confessed all my sins to you
> and stopped trying to hide my guilt.
> I said to myself, "I will confess my rebellion to the LORD."
> And you forgave me! All my guilt is gone.
> (Psalm 32:1-5, NLT)

These words were written by a man who had walked and talked with God since childhood. He had known God's blessing and power in his life. But for twelve torturous months, he had fought the conviction of the Holy Spirit and was not experiencing God's presence as he had before.

He was in relationship with God, yes, but not in fellowship. And it was hell on earth for David. One paraphrase renders Psalm 32:4 like this:

> The pressure never let up;
> all the juices of my life dried up.[62]

The king's very life—everything that made David, David—was drying up like parched clay. Every bit of the joy and hope and excitement he had once known had drained out of his soul.

God will simply not allow His child to get away with sin. If you take away nothing else from this chapter, please mark that! David's tortured soul and the searing conviction he felt in his life were really signs of life. The discipline he was enduring was a sign that he was a child of God.

> If God doesn't discipline you as he does all of his children, it means that you are illegitimate and are not really his children at all. Since we respected our earthly fathers who disciplined us, shouldn't we submit even more to the discipline of the Father of our spirits, and live forever?
>
> For our earthly fathers disciplined us for a few years, doing the best they knew how. But God's discipline is always good for us, so that we might share in his holiness. No discipline is enjoyable while it is happening—it's painful! But afterward there will be a peaceful harvest of right living for those who are trained in this way. (Hebrews 12:8-11, NLT)

If you start to go the wrong way, find serious roadblocks in your path, and feel the heat of conviction kicking in, rejoice! And if you feel the vise of guilt and remorse closing in on you after you sin, celebrate that! All of these signs are indicators that you are indeed a child of God. I have neither the privilege nor the right to discipline someone else's child, but I must discipline my own children for their own good!

David had tried to cover up his tragic sins, but the evidence of his crime was everywhere. The Bible tells us, "He who covers his sins will not prosper, but whoever confesses and forsakes them will have mercy."[63]

I have personally witnessed this so many times. You see someone who seems to have their life together, walking with God and serving Him. But for some reason, the Lord doesn't seem to be blessing their life or ministry. It's one problem after another, crisis after crisis, really of their own making.

Then one day it all comes out. You find out they have been living a lie. And make no mistake about it, sooner or later your sin will find you out! It will catch up with you.

So one day in David's life the best thing that could possibly have happened, happened.

David got busted.

The prophet Nathan came to pay the king a visit. It's significant to note that the Bible says, "Then the LORD sent Nathan to David." When? Right after the act of adultery with Bathsheba? No. Right after Bathsheba revealed she was pregnant? No. Right after David had Bathsheba's husband sent to die? Again, no.

It was about twelve months after all this had taken place, and David could hardly live with himself. The prophet tells a parable about a man who had his lamb stolen.

> "There were two men in a certain town, one rich and the other poor. The rich man had a very large number of sheep and cattle, but the poor man had nothing except one little ewe lamb he had bought. He raised it, and it grew up with him and his children. It shared his food, drank from his cup and even slept in his arms. It was like a daughter to him.

> "Now a traveler came to the rich man, but the rich man refrained from taking one of his own sheep or cattle to prepare a meal for the traveler who had come to him. Instead, he took the ewe lamb that belonged to the poor man and prepared it for the one who had come to him."

> David burned with anger against the man and said to Nathan, "As surely as the LORD lives, the man who did this deserves to die! He must pay for that lamb four times over, because he did such a thing and had no pity."

> Then Nathan said to David, "You are the man!"
> (2 Samuel 12:1-7, NIV)

David had become caught up in the story and felt hot anger toward that selfish rich man who had no pity. Who was this horrible person who would steal a poor man's ewe lamb? The fellow didn't deserve to live!

In so saying, David slipped his neck right into Nathan's noose. Strange how David could be so harsh toward a man who had merely stolen a sheep, when he had taken a man's wife and had that man killed.

Have you ever noticed that when you excuse sin in your own life, you become very critical of the very same thing in other people? This is what Jesus was referring to when He spoke of a speck in your brother's eye and a log in your own.[64]

Imagine how David must have felt when Nathan pointed a long, bony finger at the king and said, "You are the man!" At that moment, his cover was blown, his sin was exposed, and the truth was out. It was a mixture of shame, humiliation—and huge relief!

Hearing this bold declaration of his sin, David said, "I have sinned against the LORD."[65]

He had that right.

Yes, he had certainly sinned against Bathsheba, Uriah, and the women to whom he was already married. But the underlying issue was that he had betrayed and sinned against God, the One who had loved him, protected him, and blessed him since boyhood.

That's why in spite of all the wrong he had done, David was still a man after God's heart. I have read about people who have been caught in adultery. These are some of the actual things they have said:

*"Nobody's perfect."*
*"Sorry, I didn't mean to hurt you."*
*"It happens to the best of us."*
*"If nothing else, I can always serve as a bad example."*
*"I'm only human."*
*"Doing stupid things is my way of making my life interesting."*
*"Everybody has the right to make mistakes."*
*"Tomorrow, no one will remember."*
*"Stupid is as stupid does."*

And then the all-time classic, *"The devil made me do it."*

If you are a child of God, the devil didn't make you do anything! Sure, Satan played a role, but he needed your cooperation. The apostle James tells us: "Temptation comes from our own desires, which entice us and drag us away. These desires give birth to sinful actions. And when sin is allowed to grow, it gives birth to death" (James 1:14-15, NLT).

There is only one correct response to being caught in sin, and David had it right. "I have sinned against the LORD!"

Nathan then gives David this sober reminder of the effects of his sin. Because of what he had done, he had given occasion for the enemies of God to blaspheme. If only we would think of things like this when we start to fall into sin. The damage to our witness, our integrity, our reputation, and to the work of Christ in our world can't even be calculated.

The prophet went on to tell David that the sword would never leave his house. And that's exactly what happened, as David faced the repercussions of his sin for years to come. The child born from this encounter between David and Bathsheba died. Then as the years passed, David's own children repeated his very behavior. One of David's sons treated his half-sister as David treated Bathsheba, taking advantage of her. Then Absalom, another of David's sons, treated his brother as David treated Uriah and became a murderer, eventually leading a rebellion against his father.

As they say, the apple doesn't fall far from the tree.

Just because we have been forgiven doesn't mean we avoid the consequences of reaping what we have sown.

In spite of all that transpired, however, David was forgiven and restored to fellowship with God. As devastating as this story sounds, David actually did make a comeback. He got right with God and ended his race well.

Is this one of the "greatest stories ever told"?

Yes and no.

No, because it's the story of failure in the life of a child of God and a great spiritual leader. In that sense, it's one of the *saddest* stories ever told. But it is a great story in that it is also about forgiveness. Yes, David paid a heavy price for his sin. But God gave David a second chance, a new beginning.

And here is something even more stunning than that.

Out of that forgiven sin—a dreadful, sordid thing that never should have happened but did—God drew out something good. Not just good for David, but for the whole world, right down to you and me.

David was from the town of Bethlehem, and Jesus would one day be born as the root and offspring of David, both through the bloodline of Mary and the lineage of Joseph. That's why Joseph and Mary went to Bethlehem to be taxed.

But here's the shocker: *Bathsheba made it into the Messianic line of Jesus Christ (Matthew 1:6).* And she wasn't the only questionable person to make it into the Messianic line. So did Tamar and Rahab, one woman who tricked her own father-in-law into having sex with her, and the other woman a professional prostitute!

So, what does this mean?

Our God is the God of second chances! I wish I could turn back the clock for the girl who has lost her virginity before marriage. Or for the guy who has been unfaithful to his wife and lost his marriage and family. Or for the person who has polluted his or her mind with pornography. But I can't do that any more than I could unscramble an egg. Having said that, however, you can stop such behaviors here and now, even as you read these words.

Maybe you've been involved in some kind of sexual sin or adulterous relationship that hasn't yet been exposed. Now is the time to repent . . . to change your mind and head in a new direction. As Jesus said to the woman caught in the act of adultery, "*Go and sin no more.*"

Every one of us has the capacity to fall in this area, and those who feel most secure and confident may be the very ones who are walking closest to the cliff.

But the *restorative* grace of Jesus Christ that pulls us out of the pit, giving us a second chance and working all things for good in our lives, is the same *protective* grace that can keep us from falling in the first place.

That's why we owe our praise "to him who is able to keep you from falling and to present you before his glorious presence without fault and with great joy" (Jude 24, NIV).

What a Savior!

## chapter nine
# Solomon's Story:
# The Foolish Wise Man

"I looked at everything I had tried, it was all so useless,
a chasing of the wind, and there was nothing really
worthwhile anywhere." —Ecclesiastes 2:11, TLB

t he next time your past tries to keep you from following
God, just remember *you're in good company*. Stories of
flawed people, people who did both right and wrong, fill the
pages of the Bible.

Some seemed to *always* get it right, like Joseph.

Others *mostly* got it right, like David.

Others *sometimes* got it right, like Samson and Saul.

Today's chapter is about a man who finally got it right at
the end of his life, after many sad and wasted years. He was
a man who tried it all. If anyone was ever qualified to say,
"been-there-done-that-bought-the-tee-shirt," it was this man.

The Bible says that as a young man he loved the Lord, yet
he became the hedonist extraordinaire, a playboy who made
Hugh Hefner look like a lightweight in comparison.

He was highly educated, yet he went on unbelievable
drinking binges. He was an architectural genius, masterminding
the building of incredible structures, and chased after women
like there was no tomorrow. What a study in contrasts!

And he was worth *billions*.

No, I am not describing some contemporary billionaire
like Bill Gates, Donald Trump, or Rupert Murdoch. Nor am
I describing some Hollywood actor like Tom Cruise, Brad Pitt,
or Tom Hanks.

This man lived thousands of years ago. Yet the lessons and experiences of his life are as current as tomorrow's newspaper. It was
he who coined the phrase, "There's nothing new under the sun."

His name was Solomon, and his is one of the greatest stories ever told.

The son of David and Bathsheba, Solomon became the king of Israel after his father's death. No one, not even David, had such incredible potential to be a great king. He was given wisdom on a scale that had never been known up to that point, and had virtually unlimited power to do good. He had a godly heritage from his father, David, who in spite of his serious lapse recovered and became indeed a man after God's own heart.

Solomon started his reign beautifully.

But the joy and beauty began to fade all too soon, as this young king with so much potential turned away from the Lord who had so richly blessed him. In Ecclesiastes, written by Solomon, we have the story of that fall.

## A Search for Meaning

It wasn't enough for Solomon to hear about right and wrong from others. Like many young people, he wanted to know for himself.

It was a tragic decision. By the time he came to the end of himself, he had thrown away a life with unbelievable potential. Here's how he began his memoirs in Ecclesiastes.

> The words of the Preacher,
> the son of David, king in Jerusalem.
> "Vanity of vanities," says the Preacher;
> "Vanity of vanities, all is vanity."
> What profit has a man from all his labor
> In which he toils under the sun?
> (Ecclesiastes 1:1-3)

Solomon liked the word "vanity"; he used it thirty-eight times in Ecclesiastes as he wrote about life under the sun. The word vanity used here is not speaking of personal vanity, as in spending too much time in front of the mirror every day. The word here, in the original, means emptiness, futility, meaninglessness, a wisp of a vapor, nothingness, a bubble that bursts.

Ecclesiastes tells us that nothing on this earth will satisfy us completely. No thing, no pleasure, no relationship, no accomplishment will bring enduring value in life.

It's like riding one of those stationary bikes. You pedal and pedal but never really go anywhere. They have high-tech ones now where you can watch a video of a road with a scenic landscape, but the fact is, you get off that bike in the very same place where you started.

Here are more of Solomon's conclusions:

Smoke, nothing but smoke. . . . There's nothing to anything—it's all smoke.

What's there to show for a lifetime of work, a lifetime of working your fingers to the bone?

One generation goes its way, the next one arrives, but nothing changes—it's business as usual for old planet earth.

The sun comes up and the sun goes down, then does it again, and again—the same old round.

The wind blows south, the wind blows north.

Around and around and around it blows, blowing this way, then that—the whirling, erratic wind.

All the rivers flow into the sea, but the sea never fills up.

The rivers keep flowing to the same old place, and then start all over and do it again.

Everything's boring, utterly boring—no one can find any meaning in it.

Boring to the eye, boring to the ear.

What was will be again, what happened will happen again.

There's nothing new on this earth.

Year after year it's the same old thing.

Does someone call out, "Hey, this is new"?

Don't get excited—it's the same old story.
Nobody remembers what happened yesterday.

And the things that will happen tomorrow?

Nobody'll remember them either.

Don't count on being remembered.
(Ecclesiastes 1:2-11, THE MESSAGE)

Well, that's certainly cheerful! Why was Solomon so depressed?

In the book of Ecclesiastes, Solomon was looking back on a life lived without God. He was reflecting on man's attempt to meet the deepest needs of human life while leaving God out of the equation.

This is ironic when you consider his life story. Here was a man who for all practical purposes was raised in a godly home, and more importantly, for many years embraced the Lord. David gave godly advice to his son, and when he was near death, he told young Solomon: "My son, learn to know the God of your ancestors intimately. Worship and serve him with your whole heart and a willing mind. For the LORD sees every heart and knows every plan and thought. If you seek him, you will find him. But if you forsake him, he will reject you forever. So take this seriously."[66]

David was saying, "Son, you can't live off your dad's faith. You need to have your own." This is something we all wish for our children and grandchildren—that our faith would become theirs, our God their God. As Ruth said to her mother-in-law, Naomi: "Your people shall be my people, and your God, my God."[67]

Initially Solomon followed his father's advice. But as time passed, the young king forgot this commitment, allowing his heart to become at first divided, and then hardened. He began to love both the Lord *and* the world. According to Scripture, however, that will never wash.

The Bible reminds us that friendship with the world is enmity with God. Whoever will be this world's friend will be God's enemy. And in this rebellion against God, much like the prodigal son, Solomon broke away from his roots, his foundation, and decided to take a crash course in sin.

He was prepared to try it all.

## Solomon's "Experiments"

Sex, drinking, partying, unlimited materialism, the finest education, entertainment, collecting art, you name it, Solomon tried it. He actually did what most people only dream of. But in the end, it all turned into a nightmare. And bear in mind that he didn't just dabble in these things; as they say in the south, he went whole hog! He thought of it as something of a research project. He had to know for himself, so he would literally try and experience it all.

No stone would be left unturned.

No possession not acquired.

No pleasure not experienced.

The irony of all of this is that *he really knew better!* Solomon had met with God early in his reign and been blessed in a special way.

> That night the LORD appeared to Solomon in a dream, and God said, "What do you want? Ask, and I will give it to you!"
>
> Solomon replied, "You showed faithful love to your servant my father, David, because he was honest and true and faithful to you. And you have continued your faithful love to him today by giving him a son to sit on his throne.
>
> "Now, O LORD my God, you have made me king instead of my father, David, but I am like a little child who doesn't know his way around. And here I am in the midst of your own chosen people, a nation so great and numerous they cannot be counted! Give me an understanding heart so that I can govern your people well and know the difference between right and wrong. For who by himself is able to govern this great people of yours?"

The Lord was pleased that Solomon had asked for wisdom. So God replied, "Because you have asked for wisdom in governing my people with justice and have not asked for a long life or wealth or the death of your enemies—I will give you what you asked for! I will give you a wise and understanding heart such as no one else has had or ever will have! And I will also give you what you did not ask for—riches and fame! No other king in all the world will be compared to you for the rest of your life!" (1 Kings 3:5-13, NLT)

God essentially offered Solomon a blank check. What would you ask for if the Lord came to you and said, "What do you want? Ask, and I will give it to you!" Because Solomon had his priorities in order (at this particular time at least), he asked for what God really wanted him to have—wisdom to lead his people.

When you boil it down, this is what prayer is really all about—bringing our will into alignment with His. Jesus said, "If you abide in Me, and My words abide in you, you will ask what you desire, and it shall be done for you."[68]

The fact of the matter is, if I'm truly living in communion with Him, and His words are at home within me, I will be asking for what He wants me to have anyway. Prayer isn't bending God my way, but my bending His way!

This is what Jesus was saying when He told us, "Seek first His kingdom and His righteousness, and all these things will be added to you."[69]

What things? Jesus had been previously speaking of the unbelievers who think of nothing more than what they will eat, drink, and wear. So essentially He is saying, "If you put My will, plan, and purposes first in your life, everything else you need will be there for you."

That doesn't necessarily mean everything you want.

But it does mean what He says . . . everything you need.

As Paul wrote, "And this same God who takes care of me will supply all your needs from his glorious riches, which have been given to us in Christ Jesus" (Philippians 4:19, NLT).

Note that he said all of your needs, not all of your greeds. As it happens, many of the things we so desperately want don't turn out to be what we thought they would be. You've heard the saying, "Be careful what you wish for, because you might get it." There's a lot of truth in that. Because God truly loves us and wants our best, there will be prayers He doesn't answer with a "Yes."

He may say, "Wait," or He may say, "No."

But whatever He says is for our highest good and His ultimate glory.

As Garth Brooks has sung, "Thank God for unanswered prayers." When God does say no, it's always for a good reason— His good reason. You may not be able to see that at a given point in your life, any more than a child will see the value of homework or vegetables. But in time, you will.

The great British preacher C. H. Spurgeon said, "When you have a great desire for heavenly things, when your desires are such as God approves of, when you will what God wills, then you will have what you like."

Yes, God answered Solomon's prayer and gave him great wisdom. Solomon's discernment was so profound that people came from around the world to sit at his feet and drink in his words. An authority no less than the Queen of Sheba, after observing Solomon's accomplishments firsthand, could only shake her head and say, "The half has not yet been told!"[70]

Even at the peak of his magnificence and splendor, however, this wisest of men had already made a series of foolish decisions that would lead to his ultimate fall.

## A Series of Compromises

### 1. He compromised his walk.

As God had promised David, his son Solomon had the privilege of building a wondrous temple in Jerusalem for the worship of the one true God. His prayer of dedication in 1 Kings 8 is stunningly beautiful. After that address, he turned to the people and said,

May he give us the desire to do his will in everything and to obey all the commands, decrees, and regulations that he gave our ancestors. . . . And may you be completely faithful to the Lord our God. May you always obey his decrees and commands, just as you are doing today. (1 Kings 8:58, 61, NLT)

But even as Solomon was uttering these true and glorious words, he was in the midst of violating them. Solomon had disobeyed God and married a nonbeliever.

Solomon made an alliance with Pharaoh, the king of Egypt, and married one of his daughters. He brought her to live in the City of David until he could finish building his palace and the Temple of the LORD and the wall around the city. At that time the people of Israel sacrificed their offerings at local places of worship, for a temple honoring the name of the LORD had not yet been built.

Solomon loved the LORD and followed all the decrees of his father, David, except that Solomon, too, offered sacrifices and burned incense at the local places of worship. (1 Kings 3:1-3, NLT)

Because the Temple had not yet been completed, the people sacrificed as their neighbors did, on the high places of the pagan gods. Tragically, Solomon followed this practice too, all the while saying that he loved the Lord.

The king of Israel had become unequally yoked together with an unbeliever, and he began to compromise his singlehearted devotion to the Lord. It's an old, old story, and one I've heard many times about relationships such as these. To keep peace in the home, it is usually the believer who makes compromises to appease the nonbeliever. And this is precisely why God tells us to "not be unequally yoked"![71]

## 2. He compromised his wealth.

Solomon began amassing a huge fortune, as people paid very large amounts of money to hear his wisdom. But as time passed, Solomon began to trust those riches more than God.

Money, as they say, is a wonderful servant, but a hard task-master. We can accomplish wonderful things of eternal value for the Lord with our money, and that is why every believer should give as God instructs. There is no excuse for withholding our giving, and it blocks God's blessings when we do.

Should people cheat God? Yet you have cheated me!

But you ask, "What do you mean? When did we ever cheat you?"

You have cheated me of the tithes and offerings due to me. You are under a curse, for your whole nation has been cheating me. Bring all the tithes into the storehouse so there will be enough food in my Temple. If you do . . . I will open the windows of heaven for you. I will pour out a blessing so great you won't have enough room to take it in! Try it! Put me to the test! (Malachi 3:8-10, NLT)

Nearly every contemporary study on the subject indicates that American Christians give an average of two to three percent of their income. And nine out of ten give nothing at all. In the passage above, God challenges His people to step out in faith and be obedient with their finances—and watch what happens!

Is your money serving you, or are you serving it?

## 3. He compromised his morality.

If it wasn't enough to marry a nonbeliever, Solomon started a collection! Seven hundred wives (can you imagine that many mothers-in-law?), and three hundred concubines on top of that. Not only was this wrong morally, but it would turn Solomon to other gods.

Scripture sternly warned against this very thing.

The LORD had clearly instructed the people of Israel, "You must not marry them, because they will turn your hearts to their gods." Yet Solomon insisted on loving them anyway. . . .

In Solomon's old age, they turned his heart to worship other gods instead of being completely faithful to the LORD his God, as his father, David, had been. . . . In this way, Solomon did what was evil in the Lord's sight; he refused to follow the Lord completely, as his father, David, had done. (1 Kings 11:2, 4, 6, NLT)

As an old man looking back on so much tragic waste in his life, Solomon wrote these words: "I set my mind to seek and explore by wisdom concerning all that has been done under heaven" (Ecclesiastes 1:13, NASB).

In Hebrew, the word translated "seek" means to investigate the root of a matter, as in doing a research paper. For all practical purposes, Solomon committed himself to research the roots of human behavior. *Why do people do what they do?* As he pursued this theme, he set aside all spiritual principles and truth and neglected both his family and the affairs of state as king. Whether it was passion, pleasure, philosophy, sex, or money, he was obsessed with finding out everything he possibly could about each.

To "explore" means to examine all sides. He was saying, "I will not only study these things, I will personally experience them."

In other words, he wanted to feel the full effects of alcohol himself. He wanted to participate in sexual immorality. He was prepared to try it all—unfettered sex, drinking, partying, unlimited materialism, entertainment, collecting art, and even great building projects. But in the end, it all turned into a miserable state of existence.

## The Failure of Education

Somewhere in this long, weary odyssey, Solomon thought that if he could obtain the finest education money could buy, it would satisfy his heart.

But it didn't. Not at all.

In spite of his vast learning, there was still an emptiness, a hole in his heart.

> I said to myself, "Look, I am wiser than any of the kings
> who ruled in Jerusalem before me. I have greater wisdom
> and knowledge than any of them." So I set out to learn
> everything from wisdom to madness to folly. But I learned
> firsthand that pursuing all this is like chasing the wind. The
> greater my wisdom, the greater my grief. To increase know-
> ledge only increases sorrow. (Ecclesiastes 1:16-18, NLT)

This is not to say it's foolish to pursue an education; it's actually a wise and prudent thing to do. Solomon's problem here was
that he looked to the pursuit of knowledge *without God*. And
when God is left out of the picture, the result will always be
empty, empty, empty.

So Solomon decided to shift gears from being an honors stu-
dent to becoming a party animal. "All right," he said. "If academic
pursuit is going to leave me empty, I'll just check my brain at the
door and party!"

> I said to myself, "Come on, let's try pleasure. Let's look
> for the 'good things' in life." But I found that this, too, was
> meaningless. So I said, "Laughter is silly. What good does it
> do to seek pleasure?" (Ecclesiastes 2:1-2, NLT)

That is why the Bible reminds us that she "who lives for pleasure is dead even while she lives," and that "even in laughter the
heart may ache, and joy may end in grief."[72]

When Solomon went after pleasure, it was no holds barred.
As mentioned, he had access to at least a thousand women. He
chased after every sexual possibility his fertile mind could dream
up, and still this emptiness persisted.

So what was next? How about hitting the bottle?

> After much thought, I decided to cheer myself with wine.
> And while still seeking wisdom, I clutched at foolishness.
> In this way, I tried to experience the only happiness most
> people find during their brief life in this world.
> (Ecclesiastes 2:3, NLT)

After a few hangovers, and maybe waking up in bed with people he had never seen before, he saw the emptiness of all that. So he shifted gears once again, and with unlimited resources at his disposal, he thought he would build the finest palaces and homes money could buy. He also planted magnificent vineyards, likely beyond anything ever seen in Israel before.

And then, after many wasted years, Solomon finally came to his senses.

Solomon had learned the bitter lessons of life the hard way. But he really had no one to blame but himself. He came to a clear-eyed conclusion at the end of his memoirs in the book of Ecclesiastes.

Among other things, he deeply regretted wasting his youth, warning others not to make the same mistake.

> Remember now your Creator in the days of your youth,
> Before the difficult days come,
> And the years draw near when you say,
> "I have no pleasure in them."
> (Ecclesiastes 12:1)

Another translation says, "Don't let the excitement of youth cause you to forget your Creator. Honor him in your youth before you grow old and say, 'Life is not pleasant anymore.' "[73]

In this, Solomon was so right.

Youth is such an important time in life. It is there, in our younger days, that we lay a foundation, establish our priorities, and dream our dreams. That is why I am so committed to reaching young people for Christ.

In some ways, it would be an easy thing for me to just kick back after thirty-plus years of ministry and enjoy all that the Lord has done. Now that I'm in my mid-fifties, I can see myself saying, "Maybe it's time to slow down a little and just focus on people my own age and older."

But I can't do that. My heart burns for young people who don't know the Lord. I don't want to be like others who curse the darkness, I want to turn on the light. With all the thousands of young people who have come to Christ at our Harvest Crusades or in one of our services at Harvest Community Church, I constantly run into them all over the country and receive many letters. I have the opportunity to hear what God has done in their lives and how He is using them, with many going into full-time ministry. As John said "I have no greater joy than to hear that my children walk in truth."[74]

Which brings us to Solomon's final conclusion about his search for meaning in life. Fasten your seat belt. Are you ready?

## Solomon's Not-So-Amazing Conclusion

> Here now is my final conclusion: Fear God and obey his commands, for this is everyone's duty. God will judge us for everything we do, including every secret thing, whether good or bad. (Ecclesiastes 12:13-14, NLT)

Solomon wraps up his book by saying, "Look, take it from a seasoned pro! Believe me, I *know* what I'm talking about here! If you leave God out of the picture—no matter what else you may have going—your life will be empty, meaningless, and futile. Do you want to have a full life, a more abundant life? Do you truly want to live out your life as a whole woman, a whole man? Well, here's your answer: *Fear God and keep His commandments.*

Sadly, Solomon threw away his whole life figuring this out. Following God was the answer all along, and deep down, I think Solomon knew that from day one.

But he trashed his life anyway.

How many times have we heard this? How many more young men and women are going to step into adulthood telling themselves that submitting to the Lord really doesn't apply to them?

How many more marriages will be destroyed? How many more children deprived of both parents? How many more lives ravaged by substance abuse? How many more people living only to consume things and never thinking of others?

God only knows.

The bottom line is, don't waste your life like Solomon did. He had the potential to be a great man, and for a time he was. But he self-destructed. You would have thought that he would have learned from the example of his father, both good and bad. But he was determined to learn it all the hard way, becoming a *summa cum laude* graduate of the school of hard knocks.

Here was the wisest man who ever walked this earth, and he lived out his life like a fool.

*Fear God and keep His commandments.*

His father told him this early on. Solomon himself proclaimed this to his people at the dedication of the Temple, yet he completely disregarded it and lived the way he wanted to live. What he initially knew intellectually, he now knew experientially.

If only we would take God at His word! If only we would obey Him—even when it's difficult. To have the courage to say "no" when others are saying "yes," and "yes" when others are saying "no."

Listen, before you know it, you will have more life behind you than before you. I hope you and I will not have wasted a good part of our lives, as he did.

We all have two major dates in our lives. You can see them on the headstone of a grave, separated by a little dash: The date of our birth and the date of our death.

We can't choose our entrance, and we can't choose our exit.

But what we do with that little dash in between is all ours.

## chapter ten
# Elijah's Story, Part 1:
# The Battle of the Gods

"Then Elijah told the people, 'Enough of that—
it's my turn. Gather around.'" —1 Kings 18:30, THE MESSAGE

We live in troubled times. Sexual promiscuity and perversion proliferate on every side. Senseless and random acts of violence fill the daily news reports. Our nation has been rocked by terrorism as we have never seen before, and experts warn us it may get worse. Far worse.

It's enough to make us want to despair at times. To shrug our shoulders and say, "There's just no hope. There's nothing the church can do—there's nothing that I personally can do—to make any kind of difference."

That thought is simply not true.

The book of 1 Kings reveals an era of Israel's history where conditions were strikingly similar to our own—and in some ways even worse.

Yet one man made a difference.

His name was Elijah.

As a prophet of the living God, Elijah had an immense task before him. This prophet entered the scene at one of the darkest, most evil times in his nation's history. His story is introduced to us in 1 Kings 17, but the chapters leading up to that passage show just how godless and depraved the spiritual state of that once godly nation had become.

Throughout history, whenever a nation or a people abandon faith in the one true God, moral breakdown quickly follows. The northern kingdom of Israel had veered sharply from the Lord's commands immediately after the rebellion that severed them from Jerusalem and the southern kingdom of Judah. And once they had rejected the Lord, everything went downhill from there.

It's not that these Israelites were atheists. They just wanted to worship other gods alongside their worship of the Lord. Somehow, they imaged they could pay lip service to the God of their fathers and yet directly disobey Him by their actions.

Why shouldn't we have it all? They reasoned. Why shouldn't we have God and our idols too? Have you ever tried to imagine how this made God feel? How would *you* feel if your spouse left you for another lover? Hurt and betrayed, no doubt. But what if he or she left you for a *mannequin?*

*You don't understand! This mannequin loves me! Besides, it never criticizes or nags me. Then again, it's a little on the quiet side, but that's why I love it!*

Is it any more ridiculous when anyone—you and I included—turn from the living God to a false one? We, too, have our idols . . . we've just made them seem a little more respectable. You can hear the grief in God's voice when He told Jeremiah:

> For My people have committed two evils:
> They have forsaken Me, the fountain of living waters,
> And hewn themselves cisterns—broken cisterns that can
> hold no water. (Jeremiah 2:13)

Every person has a god—some altar he bows before, some philosophy he lives by, some pursuit, possession, or passion he gives his allegiance to. Some worship their bodies, some their intellects. But the greatest physique will eventually fail. The most brilliant mind will fade.

Others bow before the altars of power, pleasure, or possessions. When it all comes down, however, is that god going to help you in your hour of need, when you are facing tragedy, hardship, and uncertainty? When you're drowning, do you call out, "MasterCard, where are you? American Express, help me!"

Israel's false gods couldn't help them, either. And that's what led to the big showdown at Mount Carmel Corral.

## Prelude to Battle

Maybe you've heard of the big boxing matches in times past, with nicknames like "Thrilla in Manila," or "The Rumble in the Jungle." These over-hyped media events couldn't hold a candle to the Battle of the Gods!

A quick historical flyover may give us some perspective before we dive in. For over one hundred years, Israel had lived under the reign of three kings: Saul, David, and Solomon. Each had their flaws, some more than others.

When Solomon's son Rehoboam came to power, the nation was ripped down the middle, dividing into a northern and southern kingdom. At the time Elijah stepped onto center stage, the northern kingdom of Israel had known more than sixty years of blatant unbelief, assassinations, betrayals, idolatry, ungodliness, and cutthroat rulers.

Now there was a new king in town, and he was the most sinful of all. His name was Ahab. He was married to an extremely wicked woman named Jezebel, who was the real power behind the throne. A rabid idolater, she introduced Baal worship to Israel, and it was only a matter of time until her husband, Ahab, followed in her course.

Jezebel's evil reputation became so notorious that her name was used many years later by the apostle John to illustrate evil seeping into the church.

> You allow that woman Jezebel, who calls herself a prophetess, to teach and seduce My servants to commit sexual immorality and eat things sacrificed to idols. (Revelation 2:20)

Ahab and Jezebel even planted a sacred grove of trees for the worship of Ashteroth, the goddess of sex and violence. This king and queen assumed they could do as they wished, openly flaunting God's standards with impunity. But God hadn't been sleeping while all this was going on. He was very aware of what Ahab and Jezebel had been doing, and He was angry!

> Ahab did more to provoke the LORD God of Israel to
> anger than all the kings of Israel who were before him.
> (1 Kings 16:33)

Of all the thousands of Hebrews in the northern kingdom, only 7,000 remained who had not bowed the knee to Baal—but even those 7,000 were so paralyzed by fear that their existence was unknown to Elijah.

Suddenly, with no forewarning or fanfare, the mighty prophet Elijah burst onto that sordid scene. His very name was a rebuke to this wicked royal couple: *My God is Jehovah* or *the Lord is my God.* In other words, your God may be Baal, but mine is the Lord!

Elijah's origins also have a bearing on the story. He was a Tishbite from Gilead, a region east of the Jordan River. The people from that part of the land were a rough-hewn lot, tough and tanned from the sun—maybe like someone from the Australian outback. I'm not saying that Elijah was Crocodile Dundee, but dressed in animals skins as he was, he must have looked out of place in the capital city.

When we think of Elijah, we immediately think of powerful miracles such as raising the dead, stopping rain, and calling fire down from heaven. We know he was bold, courageous, and full of faith. We might say, "What good is it to look at a man like this? What principles could I possibly learn from his life to apply to my own? He was superhuman!"

But that's simply not true. James reminds us that "Elijah was as human as we are. . . ."[75] He had moments of marvelous courage and determination. But there was also a time in his life when he became so afraid, so despondent, that he wanted to give up and die! Scripture records his story to remind us once again that God can and does use imperfect people, and that it's possible to live a godly life in an ungodly world, even if it seems like we're standing alone.

Seemingly out of nowhere, the prophet strode into the palace of King Ahab and walked right up to the throne.

And Elijah the Tishbite, of the inhabitants of Gilead, said to Ahab, "As the LORD God of Israel lives, before whom I stand, there shall not be dew nor rain these years, except at my word." (1 Kings 17:1)

Elijah flung down the gauntlet of his challenge at the very nerve center of the country and his people. Where did he get such boldness? We all know how difficult it can be to stand up for something that isn't popular, to go against the grain.

No one in King Ahab's court knew anything about Elijah at that point. He just walked in off the street, following no protocol, putting forward no introductions, and making no attempt to show deference to the king. Suddenly there he was, with fire in his eyes: a rugged, rough-around-the-edges, unsophisticated man from the outback of Gilead. Everyone must have stared in open-mouthed amazement. I can see the people around Ahab asking each other, "How did this guy get through security? Where did this wild man get such boldness?"

As time went on, the rulers of the northern kingdom would become even more curious. Who was this man, and how did he come by such confidence and power? Within the story itself, Scripture reveals a number of his secrets.

## What were Elijah's secrets?

### 1. He knew God.

He stood continually in the presence of God.

As the LORD God of Israel lives, before whom I stand . . . (1 Kings 17:1)

Elijah served a living God, not a dead one like Ahab and Jezebel. Like Job he could say, "I know that my Redeemer lives. . . ."[76] The expression "Before whom I stand" is an interesting one. Though Elijah stood in the physical presence of Ahab, he was also supremely conscious of the presence of God. He understood what it meant to "dwell in the secret place of the Most High and abide under the shadow of the Almighty."[77]

When you stand in the presence of God, you will not bow before any man. The Bible says, "The wicked flee when no one pursues, but the righteous are bold as a lion."[78]

This awareness of God's presence gave Elijah the courage to stand his ground. We need to remember that wherever we go and to whomever we speak, God is with us! Elijah may have only been one person, but he was one person with God.

Do you ever feel that way? Like you are an army of one? The only person in your class, workplace, neighborhood, family who is an outspoken Christian? If so, are you willing to take a stand like Elijah did?

It's so easy even as a Christian to just blend into the wood-work. You don't want to come off as a prude, so you try to roll with it. You laugh at that dirty joke along with everyone else. You wink at an indiscretion for fear of coming off too goody-goody. You tell a lie to get that promotion, or make a compromise to be with the "in" Crowd.

But at what cost?

Elijah was no compromiser. God is looking for men and women today who are willing to stand up like Elijah. To stand in the gap.

In the book of Ezekiel, God told the prophet:

So I sought for a man among them who would make a wall, and stand in the gap before Me on behalf of the land, that I should not destroy it; but I found no one. (Ezekiel 22:30)

As Chuck Swindoll observed, "Those who find comfort in the court of Ahab can never bring themselves to stand in the gap with Elijah."

## 2. He was a man of prayer.

Elijah was as completely human as we are, and yet when he prayed earnestly that no rain would fall, none fell for the next three and one half years! Then he prayed again, this time that it *would* rain, and down it poured and the grass turned green and the gardens began to grow again. (James 5:17, TLB)

It was Elijah's prayer in private that was the source of his power in public. Notice that Scripture says he prayed *earnestly.* When we see him on Mount Carmel, praying for God to break the drought and send rain, it was not a casual, laid-back request, "Well, God, it would sure be nice if it would rain." Rather, he passionately poured out his heart to heaven. While the words he prayed are not recorded, there was an indication of his intensity in his physical posture.

Elijah climbed to the top of Carmel, bent down to the ground and put his face between his knees. (1 Kings 18:42, NIV)

Much of our prayer has no power in it because there's no heart in it! If we put so little heart in offering our prayers, we can't expect God to put much heart into answering them.

## 3. He faithfully delivered the message.

As society has changed over the last ten or twenty years, much of what we believe and declare about our Lord Jesus Christ has become "politically incorrect."

The Bible as absolute truth? *Outrageous.*

Jesus as the only way to God? *Narrow-minded!*

Clear standards of right and wrong? *Bigoted.*

The reality of heaven and hell? *Hate speech!*

The gospel is not a popular, culturally-approved message in twenty-first century America. But if we intend to be faithful to God, this is the very message we must proclaim—with as much grace, compassion, and discernment as we can. As Paul tells us:

Let your speech always be with grace, seasoned with salt, that you may know how you ought to answer each one. (Colossians 4:6)

We're to be gracious and kind, yes, but it is not for us to edit the gospel or God's Word to make it more "palatable." Paul said he did not fail to declare the whole counsel of God.[79] We cannot promise God's forgiveness without speaking of repentance. We cannot offer the hope of heaven without warning about hell. Moody said whenever you preach on hell you should always do so with tears in your eyes.

## 4. He was a man of faith and obedience.

After delivering the message of judgment to what must have been a stunned and incredulous Ahab, Elijah turned on his heel and walked straight out of the palace.

I can just imagine him stepping outside and saying, "That went great, Lord! What's next? How 'bout we take on those false prophets up on Mount Carmel?" And God replies, "Actually, I had a different plan in mind."

> Then the word of the LORD came to him, saying, "Get away from here and turn eastward, and hide by the Brook Cherith, which flows into the Jordan. And it will be that you shall drink from the brook, and I have commanded the ravens to feed you there."

> So he went and did according to the word of the LORD, for he went and stayed by the Brook Cherith, which flows into the Jordan. (1 Kings 17:2-5)

God wanted Elijah to disappear from the scene for a while. He directed the prophet to a little hidden ravine, to rest there and await further orders. To Elijah's credit, he offered no argument. He obeyed the Lord and slipped into total obscurity.

This is why God could so mightily use this man. He obeyed even if it didn't make sense in the moment. Perhaps this has happened to you. God has changed the course your life is taking. You may have left a successful career to spend more time with your young children. There may have been a cutback at work, and you were let go. Perhaps the Lord has redirected your ministry. He directed you to leave an effective work to start another.

Maybe sickness has altered your plans, or you don't have the energy you once did and have had to make changes.

This may seem like The End, but it may be a New Beginning!

When God closes one door, He always opens another. We are always ready to follow when it's green pastures and still waters, but when one of those valleys-of-the-shadow appears before us we may panic and want to find another way.

At first, hiding in the ravine must have felt strange—maybe somewhat bizarre—for Elijah. There he was sitting alone by a brook day after day, waiting for the ravens' food service to deliver his breakfast and supper. I'm sure the isolation had its drawbacks. But I have a hunch Elijah knew the Lord was prepping him for something big up ahead.

And He was.

It would be Elijah's biggest test yet. The Lord was about to challenge the false gods of Israel in a direct confrontation before the watching eyes of the nation, and Elijah was going to be His representative!

> And it came to pass after many days that the word of the LORD came to Elijah, in the third year, saying, "Go, present yourself to Ahab, and I will send rain on the earth."
> (1 Kings 18:1)

After Elijah's bold announcement and the drought that followed, he became a wanted man. His face was on every post office wall and milk carton in Israel. He had been MIA, but now he was back in action.

Elijah and Ahab had their second face-to-face confrontation, and it was every bit as tense as the first one.

> Then it happened, when Ahab saw Elijah, that Ahab said to him, "Is that you, O troubler of Israel?"
>
> And he answered, "I have not troubled Israel, but you and your father's house have, in that you have forsaken the commandments of the LORD and have followed the Baals.

Now therefore, send and gather all Israel to me on Mount
Carmel, the four hundred and fifty prophets of Baal, and
the four hundred prophets of Asherah, who eat at Jezebel's
table." (1 Kings 18:17-19)

The word Ahab uses for *troubler* means "viper, snake in the
grass." King Ahab was saying "You snake in the grass, where have
you been keeping yourself?"

I'm not too sure I would say something like that to a person
who could call fire down from heaven! Elijah could have responded, "Oh yeah, well you're toast, Ahab!"

Instead, with courage and great dignity, Elijah turned the insult back on Ahab, where it truly belonged. "I'm not the troubler
of Israel, but *you are*!" He reminded the king of how he and his
people had brought this calamity on themselves by their penchant
for full-tilt idolatry, worshipping Baal and Ashteroth.

It's always amazing to me how people will break God's commandments over and over, stubbornly resisting His loving warnings, and then when hardship comes into their lives (usually
of their own making) they blame it on God! Instead of taking
responsibility for what they have done and how they have lived,
they want to point their finger at heaven.

And of course, they take it out on God's people. "You're a
Christian? Well, let me tell you how God messed up my life. . . ."
It's really a sad situation, because these people are blaming the
only One who can help them.

None of this should surprise us. The Bible never promised us
a rose garden in this life. Paul wrote, "Yes, and all who desire to
live godly in Christ Jesus will suffer persecution."[80] In the Sermon
on the Mount, Jesus said: "God blesses you when people mock
you and persecute you and lie about you and say all sorts of evil
things against you because you are my followers. Be happy about
it! Be very glad! For a great reward awaits you in heaven."[81]

So Elijah issued God's challenge, proposing that Ahab and the
prophets of Baal and Ashteroth meet him on the peak of Mount
Carmel—with the whole nation watching!

This would be something much weightier than any heavy-weight championship between mortal men. This was to be a battle of the gods, determining who was the true ruler of the universe . . . the Lord God of Israel or Baal.

This really wasn't to be a contest between Elijah and Ahab, but between God and Satan, light and darkness, good and evil. The king of Israel agreed to Elijah's terms and assembled the false prophets on Mount Carmel—calling out the whole nation to witness the event. Perhaps Ahab thought the drought might be broken as a result of the big doings up on Carmel. It could even be that he was hedging his bets . . . if God didn't come through, he might have reasoned, maybe Baal would send the rain.

The fact is, God was positioning the evil king to step into a trap. Scripture tells us that God moves the king's heart wherever He wants.[82]

The contest Elijah proposed was to be a straightforward test. Elijah would place a sacrifice on an altar to the Lord, and the prophets of Baal would do the same for their god. The god who answered by raining fire down from heaven on the sacrifice was the true and living God . . . the Genuine Article. It was more than a fair proposal, because Baal was supposedly the god of the sun and of the elements (even though he had failed to bring rain).

As the prophet surveyed the huge crowd at the summit of the 1,600-foot peak, he laid down a challenge. "How long will you falter between two opinions? If the LORD is God, follow Him; but if Baal, follow him."[83]

Even the true believers in Israel weren't willing to take a stand at this point. When this man of God spoke of faltering between two opinions, the picture is one of someone tottering back and forth, much like a person who is intoxicated.

It's not that the people didn't believe in the Lord God of Israel. They just wanted to believe in Baal and Ashteroth too. They wanted to straddle the fence and enjoy the best of both worlds. You see, it was unpopular to worship the Lord in that day and age. The king and queen did not approve. Besides, if you just went along with the Baal-Ashteroth program, there were benefits.

If, however, you insisted on worshipping the God of Abraham, Isaac, and Jacob, you could lose your head.

The Israelites of Elijah's day didn't want to live under God's absolutes, with all the responsibilities that would bring, so they would follow some other god until things turned so bad they began to reap the results of their idolatry. Then they would turn back to the true God again. Each time they edged their way back from the brink of destruction God was merciful to them, forgiving them.

Moses saw the same tendency when the people worshipped the golden calf out in the wilderness. At one point he cried out, "Who is on the LORD's side? Let him come to me."[84] Joshua similarly realized a decision had to be made, and that a man or woman couldn't live in two worlds at the same time.

> Serve the LORD! And if it seems evil to you to serve the LORD, choose for yourselves this day whom you will serve, whether the gods which your fathers served that were on the other side of the River, or the gods of the Amorites, in whose land you dwell. But as for me and my house, we will serve the LORD. (Joshua 24:14-15)

Jesus said essentially the same thing: "He who is not with Me is against Me, and he who does not gather with Me scatters abroad."[85]

It's no different today; there are still people who try to live in two worlds. It reminds me of swimming in a lake or the ocean when the water is cold. If you're going to swim at all, it's easier to just plunge in, rather than submerging yourself inch by freezing inch. Being in that "in-between" state is the most miserable of places.

Jesus said it like this to the church at Laodicea: "I know all the things you do, that you are neither hot nor cold. I wish that you were one or the other! But since you are like lukewarm water, neither hot nor cold, I will spit you out of my mouth!"[86]

Know this: Idols in our hearts cause God to refuse to listen to our prayers. The Lord told the prophet Ezekiel, "Son of man, these leaders have set up idols in their hearts. They have embraced things that will make them fall into sin.

Why should I listen to their requests?"[87]

Finally, the stage was set.

The audience was in place.

The time had come for the battle of the gods.

## The Battle That Wasn't

> So they took the bull which was given them, and they prepared it, and called on the name of Baal from morning even till noon, saying, "O Baal, hear us!" But there was no voice; no one answered. Then they leaped about the altar which they had made.
>
> And so it was, at noon, that Elijah mocked them and said, "Cry aloud, for he is a god; either he is meditating, or he is busy, or he is on a journey, or perhaps he is sleeping and must be awakened." So they cried aloud, and cut themselves, as was their custom, with knives and lances, until the blood gushed out on them. And when midday was past, they prophesied until the time of the offering of the evening sacrifice. But there was no voice; no one answered, no one paid attention. (1 Kings 18:26-29)

Elijah almost seemed to be enjoying himself here. He was definitely having some fun at their expense, and began to mock them. The phrase "he is busy" seems to imply that Baal had taken a trip to the celestial men's room, or as the Living Bible puts it, maybe "he's out sitting on the toilet!" Now that's just flat-out funny!

But it was no laughing matter to the four hundred prophets of Baal. Why didn't their god hear them? Why didn't he answer? Almost as if they were taking Elijah's advice, they began to shout louder and louder.

Elijah wasn't the only one mocking them that day. Their own gods mocked them. Ahab and the people saw this too— the emptiness and futility of these gods the people had followed!

Sometimes when people are living in sin, they're happy there. Or at least they say they are. But as C. S. Lewis observed, "Even atheists have moments of doubt." The Bible teaches that non-Christians are blinded by the god of this world. We need to pray that God would open their eyes to reality—to their real state. They may think they are happy, but they are also on the way to hell. And if they will be honest, their so-called happiness is a shallow sort of thing, and short-lived at best.

The Israelites had to see the futility of their own gods before they turned to the Lord. Elijah allowed the false prophets to have their shot all day long—morning to evening. This hoarse, beaten, bloodied bunch had come to their wit's end. It must have been grotesque to see all those men groveling on the ground, screaming, moaning, and bleeding.

This is the world in all its glory and splendor! Satan can make a God-rejecting life seem so smart and sophisticated, so appealing, glossy, and attractive. But underneath it is filthy, destructive, and in the end . . . just plain pathetic.

With the time for the evening sacrifice coming on, Elijah stepped onto center stage.

> Then Elijah said to all the people, "Come near to me." So all the people came near to him. And he repaired the altar of the LORD that was broken down. And Elijah took twelve stones, according to the number of the tribes of the sons of Jacob. . . . Then with the stones he built an altar in the name of the LORD; and he made a trench around the altar large enough to hold two seahs of seed. And he put the wood in order, cut the bull in pieces, and laid it on the wood, and said, "Fill four waterpots with water, and pour it on the burnt sacrifice and on the wood." Then he said, "Do it a second time," and they did it a second time; and he said, "Do it a third time," and they did it a third time. So the water ran all around the altar; and he also filled the trench with water. (1 Kings 18:30-35)

Why did Elijah soak the altar three times? Because he wanted there to be no doubt when God answered and set the sacrifice aflame.

Then Elijah lifted a simple prayer to the Lord. There was no screaming, dancing, moaning, bleeding, or theatrics. Elijah had a serene confidence in God's power. This reminds us that when we are in prayer and worship, we don't have to work ourselves up into some kind of frenzy to bring God's power down.

God is already here.

He dwells among His people.

He tells us that where two or three are gathered together in His name, He's right there in their midst. Scripture reminds us that He inhabits the praises of His people.[88] In other words, when we are praising Him, He is there . . . as someone has said, "Closer than hands or feet, closer than breathing."

When we work so hard to bring God close to us, many times it's just our attempt to have an emotional experience where we can "feel" God.

Don't get me wrong. Emotions are great, and when the Lord touches you in that way, there's nothing like it. But you should never approach worship expecting such an experience every time, or conclude that you haven't encountered God because you haven't "felt" God. Just relax, know He is there, call upon Him, and let the emotions fall where they will.

God is here, and that is all that really matters.

And He was there that day on Mount Carmel, too, ready to answer Elijah's calm, dignified prayer. All of Israel was about to see a demonstration of His power.

## The Fire Falls

At the usual time for offering the evening sacrifice,
Elijah the prophet walked up to the altar and prayed,
"O LORD, God of Abraham, Isaac, and Jacob, prove today
that you are God in Israel and that I am your servant.

Prove that I have done all this at your command.
O Lord, answer me! Answer me so these people
will know that you, O Lord, are God and that you
have brought them back to yourself."

Immediately the fire of the Lord flashed down from
heaven and burned up the young bull, the wood, the
stones, and the dust. It even licked up all the water in
the trench! And when all the people saw it, they fell face
down on the ground and cried out, "The Lord—he is
God! Yes, the Lord is God!" (1 Kings 18:36-39, NLT)

This truly is one of the greatest stories ever told!

And what do we learn from this man, Elijah—the man
Scripture says was just like us? What were the secrets of
His effectiveness?

Let's review them one more time.

*He knew God.* No matter where he was, whether in the
palace of a godless king or sitting all alone by the brook Cherith
as the long days of waiting slipped by, Elijah knew he was in
the immediate presence of God. What confidence he drew
from this assurance! Who could intimidate him when he stood
in the continual presence of the Almighty?

*He was a man of prayer.* He prayed earnestly, putting
it all on the line, and God answered.

*He faithfully delivered the message.* Elijah had a tough
message from God in tough times. And he declared it just
the way he heard it.

We, too, have a message to deliver—and marching orders
from our Commander-in-Chief. It is not for us to update,
popularize, or edit the gospel of Jesus Christ. We are to
faithfully deliver it, plain and simple. And with love.

*He was a man of faith and obedience.* Elijah knew how to
occupy a place of prominence, and also how to step out of the
spotlight and patiently wait for God to act. What does that say
to you and me? Be obedient to what the Lord has set before
you today, and He will give you more to do tomorrow.

Perhaps as you read these words you realize that your passion in life—your "god," your idol—no longer satisfies as it once did. It's empty, even mocking you! There is no better day than today to call on the true and living God who loves you, giving Him a chance to answer the deepest needs in your life.

How will He answer? He may answer dramatically—with a great surge of relief, happiness, and emotion. Then again, the answer may come as a quiet confidence that grows and blossoms with the passing of time.

Either way, He *will* answer the truly searching person who comes to Him! Jesus said, "All that the Father gives Me will come to Me, and the one who comes to Me I will certainly not cast out."[89]

## chapter eleven

## Elijah's Story, Part 2: The Legacy of a Life

"Do you know that the LORD is going
to take your master from you today?"

"Yes, I know," Elisha replied,
"but do not speak of it." —2 Kings 2:3, NIV

i t seems the older you get, the faster time flies by.
When I was in elementary school, time seemed to crawl
like a snail. *When would the day be over? When would we
get Christmas break? When would summer vacation start?*

Now, it's not just the years that zip by, it's entire decades!
I read an interesting thing about what time it is in your life.

It goes like this:

If your age is 15, the time is 10:25 a.m.

. . . 20, the time is 11:34 a.m.

. . . 25, the time is 12:42 p.m.

. . . 30, the time is 1:51 p.m.

. . . 35, the time is 3:00 p.m.

. . . 40, the time is 4:08 p.m.

. . . 45, the time is 5:15 p.m.

. . . 50, the time is 6:25 p.m.

. . . 55, the time is 7:34 p.m.

. . . 60, the time is 8:42 p.m.

. . . 65, the time is 9:51 p.m.

. . . 70, the time is 11:00 p.m.

I don't know where that puts you, but for me it's about 7:30 p.m.
That's sad, because I've been going to bed at 9:30 these days!

Now that I'm a grandfather, it reminds me I have passed to
another generation. But I am determined to be the *fun grandpa*
for my grandbaby Stella (and others).

Have you heard about some of the telltale signs that age might be creeping up on you? You know you are getting old when . . .

. . . your mind makes commitments your body can't keep.

. . . the little gray-haired lady you help across the street is your wife!

. . . everything hurts, and what doesn't hurt doesn't work!

. . . your little black book contains names ending only in M.D.

. . . you dim the lights for economic reasons, rather than romantic ones.

. . . your back goes out more than you do.

. . . your children begin to look middle-aged.

. . . you are warned to slow down by a doctor instead of a cop.

. . . your knees buckle and your belt won't.

. . . you have too much room in the house and not enough in the medicine cabinet.

. . . you sink your teeth into a juicy steak and they stay there.

Why am I bringing up all these cheerful things? Because in this chapter, we will be looking at the legacy of a life.

## High Drama

As my parents' generation passes and my generation enters its final stage, we need to think about our legacy, our heritage, what we are passing on.

In one of the "greatest stories ever told," this chapter will consider the account of one man who passed his legacy to another. This is the story of the final days in the life of Elijah the prophet— and his departure was as dramatic as his entrance!

Elijah didn't just step onto the scene in Israel, he *burst* onto the scene—seemingly out of nowhere. His startling appearance and bold warnings shook up the godless status quo in the northern kingdom.

Elijah was a hairy, rough-hewn character who wore a leather belt and didn't back down to anybody. And when his work was over, God swept him up to heaven in a chariot of fire.

In what was probably his finest moment, Elijah stood boldly on the peak of Mount Carmel and yelled out to the people, "How long will you stagger between two opinions?" At the climax of that story, the fire of God fell in a dramatic fashion, and after three years of devastating drought, the rain returned—in buckets!

In spite of these great events, however, King Ahab and Queen Jezebel refused to turn to the Lord. Instead of being moved by the great miracle of fire from heaven, Jezebel only became firmer in her unbelief. Although given ample opportunity to turn from her evil ways, she only dug her heels in deeper. Like Pharaoh, she became harder each day until she paid the ultimate price—she was thrown out of a high window to her death. (Which is precisely what the Bible tells us . . . sin pays a wage, and that wage is death).

Then there was the puppet king, Ahab. He was a lot like the fickle crowds on Mount Carmel, sliding back and forth between two opinions. On the one hand, Ahab was impressed with the miracles of Elijah. But on the other hand he was afraid to offend his wicked, manipulative wife. Ahab was ultimately killed on the battlefield—in disguise—manipulating to the very end. There are so many like Ahab who are impressed by God, yet are afraid to take a stand lest they offend someone.

Ahab witnessed "the battle of the gods" we looked at in the previous chapter, and then hightailed it back to his palace—in a driving rain.

But what happened to Elijah in the aftermath of that stunning victory? Did he celebrate? Relax? No, after such a great struggle, the prophet suddenly became vulnerable.

## A Low Moment and a New Friend

As Scripture says, "Elijah was as human as we are."[90] After his great victory over the false prophets of Baal on Mount Carmel, Elijah allowed his fears to get the best of him. On word of a threat from Jezebel, he fled for his life into the desert, crawled under a scraggly tree, and asked God to take his life.

But God didn't condemn His battle-weary servant. Instead, He led him to a cave in a mountain . . . and an unforgettable experience of meeting with God.

Low lows often come after high highs.

Up in that cave, the Lord told Elijah his ministry was now coming to a close. His work was almost done, and he was about to leave the scene. But before Elijah's departure, he had to find someone to carry on the work God had called him to. It was time to pass the baton.

The Lord already had that successor picked out. Elijah was to anoint Elisha to take his place.

> So he departed from there, and found Elisha the son of Shaphat, who was plowing with twelve yoke of oxen before him, and he was with the twelfth. Then Elijah passed by him and threw his mantle on him. And he left the oxen and ran after Elijah, and said, "Please let me kiss my father and my mother, and then I will follow you."
>
> And he said to him, "Go back again, for what have I done to you?"
>
> So Elisha turned back from him, and took a yoke of oxen and slaughtered them and boiled their flesh, using the oxen's equipment, and gave it to the people, and they ate. Then he arose and followed Elijah, and became his servant. (1 Kings 19:19-21)

Yes, Elisha was a servant to the prophet. But I have a hunch they became close friends, as well. How gracious the Lord is to provide us with fellowship and friendship in those seasons of life when we're battle-weary. That's a reminder that discouragement and depression should not keep us isolated from our brothers and sisters in Christ. That's the time when we need them most!

In the season before Elijah's dramatic homegoing, the older prophet would spend a great deal of time with Elisha, preparing him for the work at hand. How important this is for us to do as well—to take all that the Lord has done in our lives and invest it in the lives of others. It's called mentoring, or to be biblical, discipling others. Yet sadly, many of us have not made this a priority in our lives.

Which brings us back to the Great Commission.

## "Go Therefore . . ."

> Then Jesus came to them and said, "All authority in heaven and on earth has been given to me. Therefore go and make disciples of all nations, baptizing them in the name of the Father and of the Son and of the Holy Spirit, and teaching them to obey everything I have commanded you. And surely I am with you always, to the very end of the age." (Matthew 28:18-20, NIV)

That is what we do across the world with our Harvest Crusades. We have all heard the "go preach the gospel" part, but we often miss the phrases "make disciples" and "teaching them."

Making disciples and teaching. Jesus first calls us to be His disciples, then directs us to lead others into the same life commitment.

Paul wrote: "So we tell others about Christ, warning everyone and teaching everyone with all the wisdom God has given us. We want to present them to God, perfect in their relationship to Christ" And to Timothy: "You have heard me teach things that have been confirmed by many reliable witnesses. Now teach these truths to other trustworthy people who will be able to pass them on to others" (Colossians 1:28; 2 Timothy 2:2, NLT).

Somewhere along the line, evangelism has been isolated from discipleship. But Jesus never made such a distinction! One should automatically follow the other. The Great Shepherd never intended for newborn lambs to be left alone in the pasture.

Next to actually leading an individual to faith in Christ, the greatest joy in life is seeing that man or woman grow spiritually and begin leading others to the Lord!

You don't have to be a Bible scholar to play a vital role in a new believer's life. For many new converts, the main problem seems to be acclimating to the Christian life. They need teaching, but they also need a personal example.

In short, they need a friend.

Later in his life, Paul demonstrated this ministry of friendship-discipling with his young associate, Timothy. In his final letter to the young man, he wrote: "But you . . . know what I teach, and how I live, and what my purpose in life is. You know my faith, my patience, my love, and my endurance" (2 Timothy 3:10, NLT). How could Timothy know those things? Only by spending time with his mentor. That was the apostle's model of bringing others along in their walk with Jesus Christ.

> And you know that we treated each of you as a father treats his own children. We pleaded with you, encouraged you, and urged you to live your lives in a way that God would consider worthy. For he called you to share in his Kingdom and glory. (1 Thessalonians 2:11-12, NLT)

Discipleship is not a new idea.

Moses did this with Joshua, Aquila and Priscilla with Apollos, Barnabas with John Mark, and Jesus with the Twelve. And of course, in the story before us, we see the same dynamic with Elijah with Elisha.

We've all heard about Simon Peter, but not as much about his brother, Andrew. Andrew never gets much press, and yet it was he who brought Peter to the Lord in the first place. If there were no Andrews, there would be no Simon Peters.

We hear about the great apostle Paul all the time. But we don't hear all that much about two men who played a key role at a crucial time in his life: Ananias and Barnabas.

These men didn't author any of the books in the New Testament, and—other than Ananias praying for Saul's eyes to be healed—they performed no dramatic miracles by the hand of God. We have no record of either of them preaching a sermon.

But both of these men touched the life of a man who in turn touched millions—perhaps billions—all over the world for two millennia! If helping Paul get started in the faith was all that they had accomplished in their whole lives, they would have still had a huge impact on the kingdom.

The fact is, we all need to be about the work of helping and encouraging those who are younger in the faith. It's important for our spiritual health. Every believer needs outflow in their lives as much as they need input. Do you know what you get when you have all input and no outlet? The Dead Sea!

We as believers could find ourselves in spiritual danger if, in our attendance at Bible studies and prayer meetings and intake of spiritual information, we do not have an adequate outlet for our newfound truths! By discipling others, we will not only save sinners from hell, we will also save ourselves from stagnation.

New believers need our wisdom, knowledge, and experience as mature believers. And by the same token, we as mature believers need their childlike simplicity of faith, their fresh love relationship with Jesus, and their zeal! As Solomon wrote, "The generous [or giving] soul will be made rich, and he who waters will also be watered himself."[91]

## A New Team Begins

When Elijah found Elisha, he threw his mantle over the younger man's shoulders.

Although Elisha may not have understood the full significance of that calling in that very moment, he definitely knew it was a big turning point in his life.

What he did next would seal the deal.

Elisha then returned to his oxen, killed them, and used wood from the plow to build a fire to roast their flesh. He passed around the meat to the other plowmen, and they all had a great feast. Then he went with Elijah, as his assistant. (1 Kings 19:21, TLB)

Elisha saw himself as a servant and an assistant to the great prophet. Did he understand that he would be Elijah's successor—and actually double his master's miraculous ministry in Israel? Elisha may have felt he wasn't quite ready for that, but in reality, he was.

Over and over again through the years, I have found that God is not looking so much for ability as availability. Someone willing to step into the gap when they see a need in the church. People often ask me how they can "get into ministry." I feel like responding, "Just look around you!" Ministry opportunities are everywhere!

As Jesus said: "Do you think the work of harvesting will not begin until the summer ends four months from now? Look around you! Vast fields of human souls are ripening all around us, and are ready now for reaping."[92]

Look at the pattern of those God called in Scripture. *They were all busy in the Lord's work already!* They weren't just sitting around contemplating their navels. When God called David to slay Goliath, he was obediently running an errand for his father. When He called Paul and Barnabas to launch out on their first missionary journey, they were already active in a teaching ministry in the Antioch church. When Philip received the call to meet the Ethiopian eunuch on the desert road, he was in the middle of a big evangelistic meeting in Samaria.

In other words, all of the people I just mentioned *were already in motion for the Lord.* The Holy Spirit didn't have to jump-start them, He just had to direct them.

So what are you doing to serve the Lord right now? Any service to the Lord—demonstrating your servant's heart and your availability—is an on-ramp to even greater service. What kind of help does your local church need? Ushering? Counseling new believers? Help in the parking lot? Giving regularly of your finances?

I'll tell you about a foreign land where you can go right away. The natives of this land are small of stature and speak a different language. The region? *Sunday school.* The tribe of people? *Little kids.*

Teaching little ones to know the Lord and follow Him is a direct fulfillment of the Great Commission. And it doesn't require a plane ticket or a passport.

## Initial Reluctance?

Understandably, Elisha at first seemed reluctant to simply walk away from everything he had known to follow the man of God. He said, "Please let me kiss my father and my mother, and then I will follow you" (1 Kings 19:20).

His words sound familiar, don't they? In fact, they are very much like the words of a man who had been called by Jesus in the New Testament.

> Still another said, "I will follow you, Lord; but first let me go back and say good-by to my family."
>
> Jesus replied, "No one who puts his hand to the plow and looks back is fit for service in the kingdom of God." (Luke 9:61-62, NIV)

Why did Jesus say that? Because He knew this man's heart through and through, and He saw the reply for what it was: an excuse to play for time. Jesus knew that once he went to say good-bye to the folks at home, he would never return. (Have you ever tried to say good-bye at a family reunion? It can take all day!)

Elijah was calling Elisha to be what *he* had been through the years: a true follower of God. As I said, he was reproducing himself. The prophet was saying, in essence, *"Elisha, if you want to be used of God, then you must make your move!"*

So it is with you. If you want to change your world, if you want to be used by God, then you must love God more than anyone or anything else! Are you willing to do that?

In Luke 14:26, Jesus said something that has puzzled many through the years: "If anyone comes to Me and does not hate his father and mother, wife and children, brothers and sisters, yes, and his own life also, he cannot be My disciple."

Obviously, Jesus wasn't counseling hatred of your loved ones here. He was saying, "Your love for God must be so strong, so intense, that all other loves in your life would be like hatred in comparison."

Elisha, realizing it was now or never, slaughtered his oxen and barbequed them on the wood of his plough. Elisha had made his commitment—and celebrated with filet mignon! There would be no looking back now. He had burned his bridges.

## Unfinished Business

With his successor chosen, Elijah could have gone into early retirement . . . a little golfing, a little shuffleboard, and maybe just kicking back on the front porch in his rocking chair. But there were still a couple of matters of serious, unfinished business that needed his attention.

Israel's wicked "first couple," Ahab and Jezebel, had passed from the scene by this point, succeeded by their son, Ahaziah. Apparently not learning anything from the Lord's harsh judgment of his parents, Ahaziah had determined to live just like all the evil kings that had preceded him.

But all his fun and frivolity came to an end with a serious accident at his palace. Somehow he had fallen through the lattice-work of an upper room, critically injuring himself. Even with his life hanging in the balance, Ahaziah refused to turn to the Lord. Instead, he sent messengers to inquire at the temple of Baal, to see if he would live.

Meanwhile, God directed Elijah to intercept these representatives of the king with a message from the true and living God. Elijah stopped them and asked, "Why are you looking to Baal to see if the king will get well? Is there no God in Israel?"

In other words, after all that happened in that nation with the three-year drought and the great "battle of the gods" on the peak of Mount Carmel, hadn't they learned anything?

It reminds me a bit of the spiritual condition of our country right now. Right after the tragedy of 9/11, people flocked to churches en masse, looking for answers and reassurance, showing (for a short season) some spiritual hunger. But now things have pretty much gone back to the way they were. Many in our nation have no time or thought for God. In some ways, things almost seem worse than before our great national crisis.

But when that next hurricane, earthquake, or terrorist attack shakes and rattles us, many will be back. History teaches one thing, and it is that man learns nothing from history.

Elijah boldly told the king's emissaries: "You go tell the king that he will die in his bed!" So much for political correctness. Elijah had certainly lost none of his boldness. So the messengers returned to Ahaziah, and the king asked them, "Why are you back so soon?"

They replied "A man came up to us and asked us, 'Is there no God in Israel? Why do you go to Baal?' " Then he said, "Go tell the king he will die in his bed!"

The king gulped. "What did this man look like?"

The messengers replied, "He was a hairy man with a leather belt."

"It was Elijah!" the king replied. Ahaziah apparently still had enough strength to become very angry, and he sent a captain with fifty soldiers to arrest the prophet.

The first chapter of 2 Kings tells the incredible story of the king's attempts to arrest the prophet, who had settled himself on a hilltop.

The captain of Israel said "Man of God, the king has said come down. . . ."

Elijah replied, "If I am a man of God let fire come down from heaven and consume you and your fifty men."

And that's just what happened. The arresting party was killed to the last man, their charred bodies lying at the base of Elijah's hill.

The exact same thing happened again! Finally, a third group came, and the captain knew he needed to take a different tack or he would be toast—literally. He basically said to Elijah, "O man of God, give me a break, I'm just doing my job!"

Elijah went with him, and then personally delivered his message to the king—face to face. If Ahaziah had been hoping for a softer answer this time around, he didn't get it. Elijah told him bluntly, "You're going to die." Age had not diminished the prophet's courage one iota. And the king died just as Elijah had said he would.

## Departure Day

When the time came for Elijah's final departure, it would prove to be a valuable time of testing for Elisha, his companion and successor. It's interesting to see how the old prophet seemed to be dissuading his disciple from coming with him.

> When the LORD was about to take Elijah up to heaven in a whirlwind, Elijah and Elisha were traveling from Gilgal. And Elijah said to Elisha, "Stay here, for the Lord has told me to go to Bethel."
>
> But Elisha replied, "As surely as the LORD lives and you yourself live, I will never leave you!" So they went down together to Bethel. (2 Kings 2:1-2, NLT)

This same exchange happened two more times: a quick trip to Jericho, and then the Jordan River. And Elisha stuck to his mentor like superglue.

Why was Elijah doing this? He could very well have been testing his disciple's commitment. Many of us will say to Jesus, "I'll do whatever You want me to do. I'll go wherever You want me to go." So the Lord tests us on that, asking us to do something difficult or go somewhere uncomfortable . . . and we begin to backpedal.

Jesus said, "You are my friends if you do what I command." And the apostle John tells us, "This is love for God: to obey his commands. And his commands are not burdensome."[93]

Whatever Jesus asks us to do, wherever He asks us to go— no matter how difficult or illogical it may seem at the time— the very best thing we can do is obey.

How would it be with Elisha? How would the apprentice fare in this test from Elijah? I think he was being given the opportunity to turn back, to change his mind, perhaps even to go home. A rough road lay ahead for Elisha. It wasn't easy being a prophet in a nation that had turned its back on God. As a highly visible representative of the living God, he would be hated and hounded by powerful people.

A similar case occurred when the fickle multitudes turned back from following Jesus. To His own disciples Jesus said, "Do you also want to go away?"

> But Simon Peter answered Him, "Lord, to whom shall we go? You have the words of eternal life. Also we have come to believe and know that You are the Christ, the Son of the living God." (John 6:67-69)

Jesus doesn't want fair-weather followers. He will intentionally thin out the ranks of those who aren't really committed. You see, God wants you to want Him. He won't force His way into your life.

Remember how the resurrected Christ appeared to the two disciples on the Emmaus Road? They hadn't recognized Him, and as they drew near the house, "He made as though He would go further . . . " before they prevailed on Him to stay.

Amazing! This is a God who responds to our invitation. That is why He gave us the ability to choose, to decide.

In Revelation 3:20, Jesus says, "Behold, I stand at the door and knock. If anyone hears My voice and opens the door, I will come in to him and dine with him, and he with Me."

He doesn't say, "Behold, I stand at your door, and if you don't open up, I'll break it down." He waits for an invitation.

Finally, just before he was to leave this earth, Elijah asked Elisha the big question.

> When they had crossed, Elijah said to Elisha, "Tell me, what can I do for you before I am taken from you?"
>
> "Let me inherit a double portion of your spirit," Elisha replied.
>
> "You have asked a difficult thing," Elijah said, "yet if you see me when I am taken from you, it will be yours—otherwise not." (2 Kings 2:9-10, NIV)

This moment was the real test of Elisha's motives and heart. What did the younger man want? Elisha simply wanted power to follow in Elijah's footsteps, faithfully and effectively carrying on his mentor's work. And God's blessing did come on him in a double portion.

What would you like the Lord to do for you today?

I heard a story about three men on a desert island who discovered a magic lamp. The genie they released from the lamp gave a wish to each of them.

The first man said, "I wish I were home with my family eating a big steak dinner." And *poof*, he was gone! The second man, encouraged by the first man's success, said, "I wish I were a billionaire living in a beautiful mansion." And *poof*, in an instant he was gone too. The third man was now all alone and feeling a bit melancholy. When it came time for his wish, he said, "I miss my friends. I wish they were still here with me!"

What do you want the Lord to do for you? Do you have a heart like Elisha, that wants more than anything else to serve God with all your heart and all your strength?

That's the kind of heart's desire that pleases the Lord, and those are the kind of prayers He delights to answer.

Elijah left a mighty legacy to his successor and friend. What kind of legacy are you leaving today? Are you discipling anyone? Do you have a life worth emulating? Or are you just a fair-weather follower?

Elijah was one of the two people in the Bible who never died (the other was Enoch). And there is a generation that will not see death, that will be caught up to be with the Lord in the air.

As the book of Hebrews tells us: "Christ was sacrificed once to take away the sins of many people; and he will appear a second time, not to bear sin, but to bring salvation to those who are waiting for him."[94]

Will you be watching and waiting like Elisha?

What a day that will be! But whether He calls us to meet Him in the air or we walk through the doorway of death, our first glimpse of heaven, our first moment in the presence of Jesus, will be—for us, forever—the greatest story ever told.

# endnotes

1  John 1:18; 6:46, NIV

2  Genesis 1:27-28

3  Luke 12:32, KJV

4  John 10:7, 9, NLT

5  John 13:1

6  Isaiah 49:15-16, NLT

7  Jude 21

8  John 16:33

9  Romans 8:31-32

10 Ezekiel 43:2, NIV

11 2 Corinthians 12:9

12 Matthew 1:23

13 Read the story in Acts 16.

14 Philippians 1:21

15 See Exodus 2:14.

16 Psalm 106:15, THE MESSAGE

17 Proverbs 14:14

18 1 Timothy 4:12

19 Judges 7:3, NIV

20 Psalm 103:14, NASB

21 See 2 Kings 5:1-19.

22 1 Corinthians 6:19-20, NIV

23 See Colossians 3:5.

24 Jeremiah 23:24

25 Numbers 32:23

26 Romans 8:31, KJV

27 NLT

28 Luke 16:11, NLT

29 See John 19:38-39.

30 Genesis 50:20-21, NASB

31 Read Jeremiah 18 for the full word picture.

32 Judges 13:5, NIV

33 Judges 13:24-25, NIV

34 Judges 14:3, NASB

35 Galatians 6:7, THE MESSAGE

36 James 1:14-15

37 1 Corinthians 15:33, NIV

38 Judges 16:21, NLT

39 1 Corinthians 10:12

40 1 Samuel 10:10

41 Acts 8:8, NIV

42 Acts 8:26-27, NASB

43 1 Samuel 16:4, KJV

44 1 Samuel 16:11

45 Psalm 27:10, NIV

46 1 Corinthians 1:26-28, THE MESSAGE

47 1 Timothy 3:6

48 1 Corinthians 1:29, NASB

49 Philippians 3:13-14

50 Luke 10:41-42

51 Matthew 6:33, NIV

52 *David: A Man of Passion and Destiny*, by Charles R. Swindoll, Word Publishing, 1997.

53 See 1 Samuel 24:7-12.

54 Romans 5:8

55 Luke 14:23, NIV

56 Ecclesiastes 3:11, ESV

57 Romans 8:15

58 Deuteronomy 17:17

58 2 Samuel 11:3, NIV

60 Psalm 141:5, NIV

61 Romans 14:13, THE MESSAGE

62 Psalm 32:4, THE MESSAGE

63 Proverbs 28:13

64 See Matthew 7:3-5.

65 2 Samuel 12:13

66 1 Chronicles 28:9-10, NLT

67 Ruth 1:16

68 John 15:7

69 Matthew 6:33, NASB

70 See 1 Kings 10.

71 See 2 Corinthians 6:14-15.

72 1 Timothy 5:6; Proverbs 14:13, NIV

73 NLT

74 3 John 1:4

75 James 5:17, NLT

76 Job 19:25

77 Psalm 91:1

78 Proverbs 28:1

79 See Acts 20:27.

80 2 Timothy 3:12

81 Matthew 5:11-12, NLT

82 Proverbs 21:1

83 1 Kings 18:21

84 Exodus 32:26

85 Matthew 12:30

86 Revelation 3:15-16, NLT

87 Ezekiel 14:3, NLT

88 See Psalm 22:2, KJV.

89 John 6:37, NASB

90 James 5:17, NLT

91 Proverbs 11:25

92 John 4:35, TLB

93 John 15:14; 1 John 5:3, NIV

94 Hebrews 9:28, NIV

## about the author

**g**reg Laurie is the pastor of Harvest
Christian Fellowship (one of
America's largest churches) in Riverside,
California. He is the author of over thirty
books, including the Gold Medallion Award
winner, *The Upside-Down Church,* as well
as *Every Day with Jesus; Are We Living
in the Last Days?; Marriage Connections;
Losers and Winners, Saints and Sinners;*
and *Dealing with Giants.* You can find his
study notes in the *New Believer's Bible*
and the *Seeker's Bible.* Host of the *Harvest:
Greg Laurie* television program and the
nationally syndicated radio program, *A
New Beginning,* Greg Laurie is also the
founder and featured speaker for Harvest
Crusades—contemporary, large-scale
evangelistic outreaches, which local
churches organize nationally and interna-
tionally. He and his wife, Cathe, live
in Southern California and have two
children and one grandchild.

# Other AllenDavid books Published by Kerygma Publishing

*The Great Compromise*

*For Every Season: Daily Devotions*

*Strengthening Your Marriage*

*Marriage Connections*

*Are We Living in the Last Days?*

*"I'm Going on a Diet Tomorrow"*

*Strengthening Your Faith*

*Deepening Your Faith*

*Living Out Your Faith*

*Dealing with Giants*

*Secrets to Spiritual Success*

*How to Know God*

*10 Things You Should Know About God and Life*

*For Every Season, vol. 2*

*The Greatest Stories Ever Told, vol.1*

*Making God Known*

**Visit:** www.kerygmapublishing.com
www.allendavidbooks.com
www.harvest.org